THE COMPUTER STUDIES SERIES

GW00717052

Business Information Systems

Chris Clare and Peri Loucopoulos

Series Editor: David Hatter

Paradigm

Paradigm Publishing Ltd
Avenue House
131–133 Holland Park Avenue
London W11 4UT

© Chris Clare & Peri Loucopoulos 1987

First published 1987

British Library Cataloguing in Publication Data

Clare, C.P.
  Business information systems. — (The
  Computer studies series).
  1. Management information systems
  I. Title   II. Loucopoulos, P.   III. Series
  658.4′038   T58.6

  ISBN 0-948825-55-3

Typeset by Mathematical Composition Setters Ltd, Salisbury
and printed in Great Britain by Hollen Street Press Ltd, Slough, Berks.

Contents

About the book

The book looks at the role and function of computer-based information systems in modern organisations. It builds on the material of other texts in the series to describe transaction processing and office systems. It discusses methods of data storage and retrieval and describes the analysis and design approaches which lead towards the most efficient and flexible information systems. Many examples are used to illustrate topics, most of them being based around the process of writing and publishing a text book.

About the series

This series of books is the first which presents an integrated approach to the complete range of topics needed by students of Computer Studies who are currently on the Higher National Certificate and Diploma courses or the first two years of a degree course.

Each volume has been so designed through its approach and treatment of a particular subject area to stand alone: at the same time the books in the series together give a comprehensive and integrated view of computing with special attention devoted to applications in business and industry.

The authors are experienced teachers and practitioners of computing and are responsible for the design of computing syllabuses and courses for the Business and Technician Education Council, the British Computer Society and the Council for National Academic Awards. In addition many of them are members of the appropriate boards of studies for the three organisations. Their combined experience in computing practice covers all aspects of the subject.

The series presents a uniform and clear treatment of the subject and will fit well into the syllabuses of the great majority of undergraduate courses.

Acknowledgements

The authors would like to acknowledge the help and useful comments provided by many students at South Bank and UMIST. In particular they appreciate the contributions of Guy Carter, Dilip Patel, Varsha Patel.

CHAPTER 1

Management information systems

1.1 Introduction

A successful business or commercial enterprise operating in the 1980s is an extremely complex system. Not only is the functional system itself a complicated set of interrelated parts, but it must also interact effectively with the outside world, the business community, central and local government, and society as a whole. In order for its operation to be effective, its management and operational personnel need up-to-date, relevant and accurate information upon which to base decisions which affect the current and future operation of the organisation. Over the last few years, senior management of successful organisations have come to regard information and the data from which it is derived as an important company resource; perhaps as important as the machinery, building and people which have always been thought of as resources vital to the operation of the organisation.

Despite this, many managers still have problems in procuring the right information in the right place at the right time. Before the advent of large-scale computerisation of information systems, the usual complaint was that of too little information upon which to base decisions. The computer revolution in commercial systems which started in the third generation (1960s) sought to put this right, but this has tended to create another problem: that of too much information. Too much information can make the life of the decision maker just as difficult as too little information since the vital 'gems' are hidden among a mass of irrelevant data.

To be effective, a modern manager needs to be able to specify only that information that he really needs and the computer should provide it either in the form of regular reports or preferably in response to *ad-hoc* enquiries made by the manager. Information is required and not data. These terms are often used as synonyms but they are, in fact, quite different and a distinction needs to be made between them.

1.2 Information and data

An important part of everyone's life is the collection of facts. This is a process which can be carried out as part of a methodical scheme or within the subconscious. If a person has to make a particular journey, certain facts have to be gathered. These may include the time of arrival, the time the journey will take by car, the time it will take by train or bus, the relative costs of these modes of transport, the weather conditions and so on. These are all facts relating to the proposed journey and are known as data.

Data on its own, however, has no real meaning. If it is to be of any value it must be given some kind of meaning or interpretation and this can only be achieved by carrying out some form of processing on the data. In the above example, the cost of the train journey is of little use until the person processes the item of data by comparing it with the cost of using the car. This piece of processing needs further refinement to take into account all the other data to result in some information concerning the best mode of transport at that particular time on that particular day. So the procedure involves:

- the collection of relevant data
- processing that data to produce a useful result

The 'result' is a pre-requisite for a decision to be taken and is known as information. The information does not actually make the decision, but merely aids the decision maker by attempting to remove as much uncertainty from the problem as possible.

It is therefore apparent that data and information are two different concepts. Data is facts collected from observations or recordings about events, objects or people. Information is the product of the meaningful processing of data which enables an individual to gain knowledge in order to be able to make a decision.

In the same way that the individual required information before deciding how to undertake the journey, so managers in an organisation require information upon which to base their business decisions. The way in which this information is generated and transmitted determines in many ways the success or failure of the enterprise.

If information is to be of any real value to the decision maker, then the data from which it is derived must be relevant and its processing must be meaningful. It would be of little use if the person making the journey were to collect data concerning the latest opinion polls on the government's popularity since this is not relevant to the problem. Of equal irrelevance would be processing the data on the cost of the rail fare to find its equivalent in Swiss francs.

Information helps the decision maker by reducing uncertainty. However, it is only of real value if it is relevant, accurate and current. Moreover, for it to display these properties, the data from which it is derived must also be relevant, accurate and current.

A modern organisation consists of a number of different parts, all of which must work together towards meeting its objectives. A typical manufacturing company will have departments concerned with production, sales, stock maintenance, purchasing, accounting, personnel and so on. Each part will perform a series of operations relevant to its particular function, but they all must interact one with another for the company to be successful. It would be useless for the sales department to sell 10 000 items each week if the production department could only output 5000. If this interaction is to be successful, information needs to be passed between the different departments; there will be many information flows throughout the organisation.

The system of information flows throughout the organisation is known as its information system. Much of this information is used by managers at all levels in order to take decisions relating to the operation of the organisation.

This information flow, that is the interaction between different parts of an organisation, is necessary in order that the organisation may function properly. Consider, for example, a manufacturing company consisting of the different functional areas of accounting, order processing, manufacturing etc., as shown in Figure 1.1. It is clear that no single function can exist in isolation but each one needs to interact with many others (as well as with the system's environment) through the flow of information.

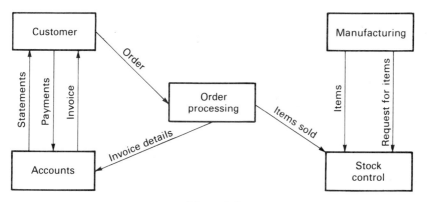

Figure 1.1

The generation of information and its flow through an organisation's different functional areas is a prerequisite for the efficient support of the operational and management structures of that organisation. However, effective use of the information can only come about if the entire process is undertaken in an orderly fashion. The mechanism which enables an organisation to achieve this is known as a (management) information system (MIS).

An information system is defined as the mechanism which provides the means of storing, generating and distributing information for the purpose of supporting the operations and management functions of an organisation.

1.3 The manager's requirement of the MIS

The term 'management' has already been referred to a number of times. If one were to seek out a definition of management from ten different sources, then ten different ones are likely to occur. Most of those definitions would, however, refer to the following functions:

Planning. Plans are made at various levels in the hierarchy of an organisation with the aim of meeting its stated objectives. There are various levels of plans covering long- and short-term periods and these will be mentioned in a later section. They concern the acquisition and use of the resources of the organisation to meet its objectives in the most cost-effective way.

Organising. Having made the organisational plans, a manager needs to organise the available resources, both material and human, into an appropriate structure for the implementation of those plans. Tasks need to be assigned, responsibilities allocated, budgets set and timescales drawn up. In doing so, the manager needs to be aware of the organisation of other departments so that his own can interact effectively.

Directing and motivating. This is the stage of actually getting the operation going. Staff need to be directed to their particular tasks, and the biggest problem that the manager faces is that of staff motivation. A great deal of research points to the fact that a participative approach to management tends to be more successful in this area since it often involves the introduction of changes of practice for the staff working in the department. An essential prerequisite for such a management style is a good communication system between manager and staff and this is an area where an effective information system can be of benefit.

Monitoring. Once the operation is underway, the manager has to keep a constant check on its progress. Targets set at the planning stage have to be met, and any variances may require corrective action. Very often those targets are quantified in the form of a budgetary control system and variances in operational or departmental budgets need to be fed back to the responsible manager by the information system.

Controlling. The feedback from the monitoring process may indicate variances from budgets which require urgent corrective action on the part of the manager. Plans may need to be modified, the organisation may need to be amended or there may be a problem of lack of staff motivation. Decisions need to be made if the operation is to be put back on course and these decisions require appropriate information.

To reiterate an earlier point, the job of the manager can only be done effectively if he has access to information which is:

- accurate
- relevant
- up-to-date

The quality of the MIS affects the quality of the information presented to individual managers and hence the quality of the decisions they make. Many people regard information as some form of power, but perhaps a better analogy would be that of a power tool. A carpenter can perform much more effectively using a sharp electric drill than with a blunt brace and bit.

1.4 The flow of information

Information is a corporate resource and should not be regarded as the property of any one department. Different departments may have distinct functional operations but these are all closely interrelated and require information from each other. Any restrictions in the flow of information between departments will adversely affect the operation of the organisation as a whole. It is no longer valid to use the approach which was typical of third-generation computer systems which sought to computerise individual functional areas. Such an approach led to problems of interfacing the individual systems, and these interfacing problems manifested themselves as restrictions in the information flow between departments. The modern approach to the design and development of information systems is to take a corporate approach and look at the whole organisation. As a corporate resource, information costs money: collecting data and processing it is an expensive operation in terms of both set-up and running costs. It should not be a resource which is managed in isolation but should, like all the other resources, be managed from the top level of the organisation.

Planning is an activity which takes place at various levels in the organisational hierarchy. A business organisation, being itself a system, will have its own goals. In order to meet these goals, the organisation has to form plans. These plans are modified as they are passed down through sub-systems but, at each stage, the plan is the pattern by which the sub-system can meet its goal.

Corporate plans. These are the definition of the company's goal — the overall objective, the raison d'être; for example, to make a profit.

Strategic plan. This takes the organisational goal(s) and translates it into long-term policies. It is the statement of how the goals are to be achieved, for example: achieve a 25 per cent return on investment per year; achieve at least $\frac{1}{2}$ million nett profit; ensure all households have a phone by 1990.

Tactical plan. This breaks down the planning a stage further to the major sub-systems of the organisation. It is usually concerned with much shorter periods and will concern itself with sales analyses and forecasts, cash-flow projections, production targets etc.

Operational plan. This is at a similar sub-system level to a tactical plan but on a much shorter timescale, such as month to month. It will concern itself with current stocks in hand, work in progress, outstanding orders etc.

The planning process at all levels involves making decisions and it has already been noted that those decisions are based on the outputs of the MIS. It follows then, that the levels of information from the MIS must correspond to the different levels of planning. It is not only the planning activity that takes place at the different hierarchical levels but also the other management functions — organising, directing, monitoring, controlling — and these also require the appropriate levels of information. The information flows which constitute the MIS therefore occur vertically through the organisation as well as horizontally.

This concept can be demonstrated by the diagram in Figure 1.2, where an organisation is viewed from the point of planning and control,[1] divided into three levels.

(1) *Strategic planning.* This is concerned with the setting of objectives in the organisation and the resources required for attaining these objectives. This management process is concerned with long-term activities.

(2) *Management control.* This is directed towards medium-term activities and ensures that the resources are obtained and used in an optimum way.

(3) *Operational control.* This is concerned with short-term activities and assures that specific tasks are carried out efficiently. It is transaction oriented, the problems are repetitious and are well structured.

The line manager's information will concern the daily output from his particular section of the factory. Middle management will require information on whether orders are being met, probably on a monthly basis. Senior management will require details on profitability on a quarterly basis.

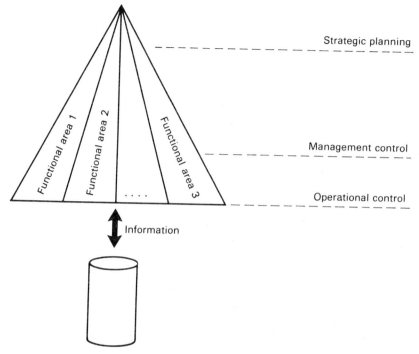

Figure 1.2

Moreover, middle and senior management will require information upon which to forecast future operations so that decisions can be made regarding future strategic and corporate long-term plans.

Managers at middle and senior level require still more of the MIS. In the same way that the individual departments are sub-systems of the organisation, so the organisation itself is a sub-system of the whole business community. The business community is a sub-system of society as a whole. There is a considerable flow of information between the organisation and its environment. Information is required which concerns the statutory accounts, market trends, consumer tastes, legislation such as the Data Protection Act and so on. A good MIS should provide information for forward planning and much of this information comes from the outside world.

1.5 Function of an MIS

Management concerns itself with making decisions, and the process of decision making is very complex, involving much intuition and subjectivity on the part of the decision maker. However, the more that uncertainty is reduced, the less the decision maker has to rely on intuition and subjectivity. Information does not itself make a decision but seeks to reduce the uncertainty. The decision-making process varies from individual to individual although very often the following process takes place:

(1) Identification of various courses of action. In the problem of making the journey, these may be to travel by car, to travel by train, to travel by bus, to travel by taxi or indeed to forget the entire journey.
(2) Building a decision rule. This is a method of specifying how the decision will be made. The traveller would probably formulate a rule which specified that he would choose the cheapest mode of transport if he woke up in time and the weather was good. The rule would become more complicated if he took into account the 'cost' of getting soaked if the weather was rainy on the day of the journey.
(3) Assessing what information is required. The traveller could always choose his mode of transport by intuition, but he may be concerned about his bank balance and he may wish to apply the decision rule rigidly. In order to do so he will need information on the 'cheapest' modes of transport (remembering that getting soaked to the skin is 'expensive') on the day of the journey.
(4) Identifying the available data. Having decided the information he requires, the traveller needs to look at the available sources of data and determine which of them are relevant to providing a basis for producing the required information.
(5) Determining the processing of the data. Information is processed data and, if it is to be of any use, that processing must be meaningful. Part of the decision-making process is to define how the data is to be processed in order to achieve the required information. The traveller would make cost comparisons of the various modes of transport, incorporating the cost of his time and the benefit of staying dry in inclement weather.
(6) Finally, the collecting of the data, processing it and applying the decision rule to the result.

The above outlines a very mechanical approach to decision making but one that is often done either consciously or sub-consciously. Managers in an organisation would have executed the above steps in order to specify the information they require and the MIS should be designed to provide it.

The decision-making process has been studied by many researchers. Simon, in his individual research and in his joint work with Newell,[2,3] established the foundations of decision-making models. Decision-making is defined as a three-stage process known as: the intelligence, the design and the choice stages.

(1) *The intelligence stage.* This stage is concerned with the identification of a problem and the collection, classification, processing and presentation of data.

(2) *The design stage.* This stage is concerned with planning for alternative solutions. If available data is insufficient for evaluating the different solutions, then more may be required from the intelligence stage.

(3) *The choice stage.* A choice is made from one of the alternative solutions. The decision maker is faced with a number of difficulties during this stage, examples being conflicting interests, uncertainty as to the outcome, multi-preference when having several variables not all of which are comparable etc.

An MIS is a system for information provision dedicated to the task of providing the management of an organisation with information on which to base their decision making. Typically, an MIS will generate several types of report:

(1) *Scheduled listings.* Produced at regular intervals and providing routine information, for example, sales figures, items produced etc.

(2) *Exception reports.* Action-oriented management reports. Generated if functional operation of the business deviates from the plans. They ignore normal events and focus attention on the abnormal.

(3) *Predictive reports.* Used for planning. Future results are forecast using planning models. Management can manipulate variables to get answers to 'what if?' type questions.

(4) *Demand reports.* Produced only on request (on-line access to computerised MIS). Can be on any aspect of the data held by MIS.

Each of these categories of output from the MIS should meet the objectives of the decision maker in respect of:

● the frequency of the decision making
● the response time required
● the degree of accuracy required
● the amount of information required

It must be re-emphasised that the MIS *assists* the decision maker and does not replace him. However, often the MIS can have various decision-making abilities built into it. A stock control sub-system may automatically generate an order for a line which falls below a certain stock level. As the degree of built-in decision making increases, the MIS becomes more a decision support system.

1.6 Types of MIS

Information systems are characterised by large volumes of data, with well-defined structures, complex interrelationships between constituent parts and distributed functions.

Present-day information systems may be broadly categorised as transaction processing systems and office systems.

1.6.1 Transaction processing systems

Transaction processing systems are deterministic and repetitious in nature and are heavily data-oriented systems.

These systems deal with the daily arrival and processing of an organisation's business transactions and are therefore the cornerstone of the entire information system.

Chapter 2 deals with issues associated with this type of system.

1.6.2 Office systems

Although some people regard an office automation system as an extension of a distributed transaction processing system, there is a significant difference. One of the major components of an automated office is an electronic mail system. This handles 'messages' between staff within the organisation, transferring them between the workstations via the local area network.

Messages, unlike transactions, are difficult to define in that

- they are of indeterminate length
- they may or may not require interaction
- they occur at random time intervals

The approach to planning an office automation system therefore differs from the planning of a transaction processing system and this is further discussed in Chapter 3.

1.7 References

1. Anthony, R. A. (1965). *Planning and Control Systems: A Framework for Analysis*, Div. of Research, Graduate School of Business Administration, Harvard University.
2. Newell, A. and Simon, H. A. (1972). *Human Problem Solving*, Prentice-Hall.
3. Simon, H. A. (1960). *The New Science of Management Decisions*, Harper.

Transaction processing systems

2.1 Introduction

The development of the MIS is an integrated approach to the organisation's information needs — it is a total system and not just restricted to a single functional sub-system. It is therefore sensible that the structure of the MIS should reflect the structure of the organisation which it serves.

The modern, fourth-generation MIS has evolved over the various generations of computing. In the beginnings of commercial data processing, computer systems were set up to undertake one specific task in one specific department: to produce payslips, to produce various invoices etc. Such systems, although crude by today's standards, produced enormous efficiencies and benefits over the equivalent manual systems. They were, however, employed to produce one type of output for one particular department.

Once the expertise in the design and development of such systems had been built up, managers began to realise that the large amounts of data, which had been collected and stored at considerable costs, could be useful to them in the form of summaries and itemised reports. For example, a payroll system could produce a breakdown of overtime worked by particular grades of staff and this could be used to determine whether more staff were needed. The next stage in the evolution was to produce these extra reports during the normal operation of the computer run. These extra reports were useful for the management of the organisation and were the equivalent of today's scheduled listings.

The next stage in the process was to make the computer system relieve some of the burden of the manager in the area of monitoring the performance of the operation. The idea of the exception report evolved, a report which would only be produced if something went wrong. Computer systems started to take over some of the more mundane aspects of management.

With the advent of reliable data communication hardware and software came the ability for the manager to enter various demands or queries of the system. Early third-generation systems could do little more than activate, on demand, certain pre-programmed reporting operations, but with the introduction of databases with sophisticated database management systems, the manager could make a range of different requests of the system and, as long as the appropriate data was held, the information could be reported.

The fourth generation saw the economic viability of distributed computer systems and the appearance of the desk-top computer. Today's systems allow a manager to develop his own decision support systems by using complex data-handling software and sophisticated graphics.

2.2 Modes of processing

The MIS is about processing data to produce information. There are a number of different ways of organising this processing and these are known as modes of processing.

A transaction is an entity that describes a particular activity carried out by an organisation. When a manufacturer deals with a customer's order, a number of transactions are generated such as: sale of goods, billing the customer, resultant payment etc. The data from these transactions must be processed so that the stock can be updated, an invoice is generated and the payment is managed.

The way in which the transaction data is collected and processed is called the processing mode.

2.2.1 Batch processing

Transactions are collected and ordered into groups (batches) and data from these are processed all together at some specific time (hourly, weekly . . .); for example, sales slips from a retailer may accumulate throughout the day, and in the evening are grouped together and passed to the data prep centre. Usually one complete batch submitted to the computer is called a job.

Although batch is often frowned upon as an old-fashioned mode of processing, it is the natural solution for many functions, for example, payroll, quarterly billing etc.

The typical batch-processing system involves, usually, the processing of the transactions against one or more master files, for example, of stock levels, of standing charges, of rental records (in BT), of employee details. A number of problems can arise from using batch processing.

(1) There is a time gap (often very large) between the capture of the data and the provision of information. A balance has to be struck between the currency of the information required and the system schedule loading.
(2) Batch requires careful schedules involving the loading of files, software, special stationery etc. This in turn requires careful scheduling of the operations staff involved.
(3) Problems are created as regards random enquiries. Operational files are usually kept offline and would have to be loaded. This process, as well as being costly, would probably give far too long a response time.

2.2.2 On-line and real-time processing

With these modes of processing, it is not necessary to batch all the transactions together before they are processed. A characteristic of such systems is the use of user terminals (VDUs) by the transaction clerks. An on-line processing mode is where a user can interact with the computer at any time via I/O channels. Transactions can be input at their point of origin. The results of the processing can be transmitted back to the user in a very fast time. If an on-line system involves the interrogation of some data (for example, an account balance), then it follows that the relevant file has to be permanently on-line. Realistically, only direct-access devices (disks) can be used for such systems.

Real-time is the processing mode where the computer accepts transaction data directly from the user, processes it, and returns the result to the user within such a time period *as to affect the user's activities or environment*. This time interval varies between one application and another: for example, stock control (10–15 minutes), missile system (?).

The two terms, on-line and real-time, are closely related and in the majority of cases the presence of one indicates the presence of the other. For example:

● warehouse serves a mail order company.
● customer orders processed by clerk on-line to computer
● order satisfied if stock file says stock in
● order processed and stock file updated
● delivery updates stock file also

Stock file is maintained on-line and updated in real-time.

From the point of view of currency, on-line–real-time (OLRT) is the ultimate processing mode. Files are updated as data arrives and subsequent enquiries reflect this up-to-date state. Also, by their nature, the operational files must be permanently accessible by user programs, and so user enquiries are easy and quick to accommodate.

OLRT has advantages over batch in that:

- users are more involved with 'computing process'
- data validated on-line and can be immediately corrected
- data conversion is avoided
- database applications can be accommodated
- reduction in printouts/hardcopy circulating
- user gets better service

Different problems of design are presented by a natural batch as opposed to an OLRT application. For example, with batch we worry about:

- how to convert data
- how to batch transactions
- when to submit batches
- who controls the process

With an OLRT application, however, consideration needs to be given to:

- work content (amount of processing for a single transaction)
- arrival pattern of transactions (batch can iron out peaks by scheduling)
- type of user and training required

The factors to consider in choosing a processing mode are:

(1) *Volume of data.* Large volumes of transaction data are usually best handled by batch; that is, do not enter 10 000 payroll transactions via terminal.
(2) *File processing.* Large serial files with applications processing most of their records are usually processed in batch.
(3) *Output details.* If the information output fits on one or two screens, then OLRT is realistic but large complicated reports may be best suited to batched output.
(4) *Response time.* The shorter the required response time, the greater the need for OLRT.

These criteria are often supplemented by other specific points relevant to particular applications. However, in many cases a hybrid approach is adopted. For example, in a financial broker's system:

- all transactions may be handled on-line
- at end of the day statements, confirmations of deals, rate changes etc. may be handled in batch mode.

As well as looking at the processing mode from the point of view of when the transactions are processed, we can also look at where the processing takes place. In other words, where the processing power is located.

2.2.3 Centralised processing

In the early days of computing, the most economic way of satisfying the information needs of an organisation was by using a centrally-located, large-scale mainframe which served all the organisational sub-systems. Economies of scale occurred in:

● operations: mounting tapes, disc packs etc.
● programming effort: the production of unified common systems which could be used by more than one of the organisation's functional units
● hardware: historically, hardware was cheaper, per transaction processed, the bigger it was

Other advantages occurred from:

● easy cross-referencing of data files
● easier management of personnel and procedures
● ease of compatibility of equipment

Centralised processing is still relevant in an organisation where the bulk of the functional sub-systems are located in the same complex. However, if the organisation is dispersed in any way, another form of processing may be more suitable.

2.2.4 Distributed processing

Changes in the economics of data-processing equipment has meant that over the past five years, distributed processing systems have become viable. A distributed system, illustrated in Figure 2.1:

● consists of two or more geographically separate computers on which applications programs can run
● uses data communications technology to link these machines together

Much of the drive towards this change has resulted from the users rather than the manufacturers. The aim was to bring the computer nearer to the

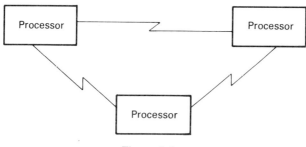

Figure 2.1

user and further away from a monolithic data-processing department. These moves have been assisted by the rapid developments in:

- computer hardware (cheaper, chip-based hardware)
- data communications (network architecture)

Each computer in a distributed system is known as a node.
Many distributed systems consist of:

- a host computer which controls the network, runs bulk programs and stores bulk data
- remote computers which undertake local processing of data

The early distributed systems had mainframe host and mini-computers as remote nodes but many now have equal-status computers linked together so that each is capable of communicating with the others. Depending upon whether or not a central node exists, control of the system may be central or distributed. Control functions include:

- handling messages between the nodes
- synchronising update operations
- recovery procedures

In a centralised control configuration, control is handled by the central computer, whereas in the fully distributed, each node operates at an equal logical level and control is performed by the node initiating the transaction. Thus the processing load can be distributed:

(1) hierarchically (Figure 2.2) where corporate data is held and processed by mainframe, accessible by local minis. Local data held and processed by local minis.

(2) horizontally (Figure 2.3) where each mini performs tasks pertinent to local needs. Should data from another location be required, the local mini communicates with the appropriate remote mini.

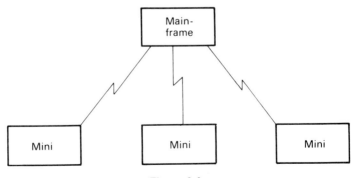

Figure 2.2

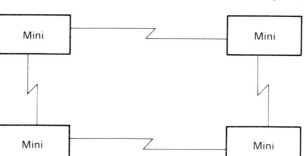

Figure 2.3

Very often, hybrids can appear (Figure 2.4).

As mentioned above, data may be shared by many different nodes. If the corporate data is dispersed among a horizontally distributed system, we have a distributed database.

The following general points relate to distributed processing:

(1) Control is vested in the user. Data-processing operations are largely the responsibility of the operational unit.
(2) Distributed systems can be developed in a modular way. Only those units needing computer power can have access to it and can access only as much as they require.
(3) Reliability factors. If one node in a distributed system goes down, much of the processing can carry on, particularly if a replicated or partitioned-by-value database is used.
(4) Some communications costs may be reduced. Local users are connected to a local site, reducing the number of 'long lines' for on-line working.

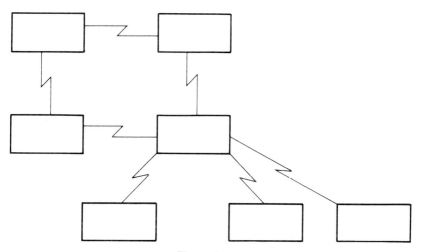

Figure 2.4

2.3 Data storage and retrieval

An information system in an organisation is concerned with the relevant processing of meaningful data. Very often this data amounts to vast quantities of material vital to the proper function of the organisation and the utmost care needs to be taken to ensure that it is kept up-to-date, accessible and secure. The data will normally be stored on the backing storage media of the installation (magnetic disc and, occasionally, magnetic tape) and this storage is not done on an *ad-hoc* basis but in the most logical and efficient way. In the same way that a manual system requires a rigorous and accurate filing system, so a computerised system requires that its storage and retrieval of data are carefully organised and controlled.

The parallels between computerised and manual treatment of data can be taken further. When people communicate with each other, they often use models to represent concepts about which they are communicating. These models are given names which are universally understood, thereby easing the communication process. For example, the object *book* can be generally understood by an English-speaking person. A picture is immediately conjured up in the mind when the term is mentioned and is used as a model during the discussion. Moreover, a concept or object is often described in terms of certain features which are important to the particular discussion. In other words, a large blue book about computing. Not all of the possible features are always used (for example, typeface, number of diagrams, paper quality etc.), only those relevant to the particular discussion taking place.

A similar practice occurs in data processing. Data concerning certain objects (customers, authors) need to be recorded and that data consists of the relevant features which are required by the information system (for example, customer's number, name, address etc.). On a more formal basis, data processing deals with *entities* and these are described in terms of certain of their *attributes*. In a large system there may be many different *occurrences* of a particular entity (a publisher deals with many customers) and each occurrence is distinguished by its own particular values of the relevant attributes, for example:

Entity	*Attribute*	*Attribute value* *(particular occurrence)*
Customer	Customer name	Foyles

The successful and efficient operation of a computerised information system stands or falls on the way in which these entities, their attributes and occurrences are recorded on and accessed from the backing storage media. The storage and retrieval of data can be implemented in a variety of ways but these fall into two basic families. The first family of methods are generally referred to as file-based systems and the second as database systems. This chapter discusses both approaches.

2.4 File-based systems

When discussing the roles and organisations of files, it is useful to define some terms. A *record* is the term used to describe a particular entity, and consists of a set of attributes which are referred to as *fields*, for example:

Record : Author

Field	Type	Size in characters
Author Code	Numeric	5
Author Name	Alphabetic	30
Author Address	Alphanumeric	100
.	.	.
.	.	.
.	.	.

This defines the layout of the record type Author. In an information system for a publishing company, there will be many occurrences of this record type, all of which conform to the defined layout. The majority of data-processing applications involve retrieving a particular record from storage and processing it in some way. This requires differentiating between one occurrence and another and this is done by looking at one or more of the values in the fields of the records. In other words, to retrieve the author record occurrence of Chris Clare, the Author Name field is accessed for every occurrence and inspected to see if its value is 'Chris Clare'. Usually, one (or more) of the fields of a record will uniquely identify a particular occurrence and usually one particular field is identified as a primary field to be used in the search for a particular occurrence. This field is known as the *key*.

The implication so far has been that records have a fixed number of fields, each of which is of a fixed size. If this is the case, the subsequent processing of records is in many ways relatively straightforward, but it can lead to a waste of space. For example, an author called Fred Ng only requires 7 of the 30 characters in the name field. Furthermore, in some applications, the number of fields can vary from occurrence to occurrence. If the Author record contained fields for each book an author published, then Chris Clare may require just one set of these fields whereas Fred Ng may require 10. Such *variable-length* records may occur when:

- the number of fields can vary
- the length of the fields can vary
- a combination of the two

When records are stored on disc or tape, it is often the case that the physical units of storage (the sector or track on disc or the block on tape) are fixed for that particular unit. These physical units may be of different

```
field value  1 ⎤
field value  2 ⎟    record occurrence  1 ⎤
field value  3 ⎬    record occurrence  2 ⎥
                    record occurrence  2 ⎬  file
field value  n ⎦    record occurrence  n ⎦
```

Figure 2.5

size to the logical record size discussed above. There is often a distinction made, therefore, between the physical record (the quantity of data input or output in a single read/write operation) and the logical record (the 'user's' view of the record).

As a final point, applications involve the manipulation of many record occurrences as part of their information system. Record occurrences of the same type are grouped together to form a *file*. This hierarchy of terms is described in Figure 2.5.

Files can be discussed in a variety of ways but perhaps the most useful are to look firstly at the part a file plays in the information system and secondly the way in which it is structured.

2.4.1 The role of files

The way in which a file is used within a computerised information system can be categorised into master files, transaction files and backup files.

Master files

Certain files of data contain records vital to the functional operation of the organisation. These files must be kept permanently up-to-date since they are in a sense the life-blood of the organisation. A publishing company, for example, cannot function unless it has accurate, comprehensive and current data on its authors, its customers, its typesetters, its printers, its advisers and so on. The accuracy, comprehensiveness and currency of this data is achieved by continuous maintenance of these files and therefore they are known as *master files*. The operation of changing a master file to reflect the latest state of its data is known as updating the master file.

Transaction files

In many applications, data is processed on transactions which have taken place during a specific time period, for example, an hour, a day or a week. This data is subsequently used to update master files during the processing and in order to ease this process the data is collected and stored on the computer as a transaction file. The transaction file is then processed and the master file updated. This is a description of a typical batch-processing system. Some applications require that a master file is updated as soon as a transaction occurs. These systems, known as real-time, do not usually involve the storing of transaction data on a file prior to processing although the transactions are often filed after processing.

For certain file organisations (Section 2.4.2) it is necessary to sort the transactions into a specific order (according to one or more key fields) prior to processing. For example, orders from bookshops may arrive in an *ad-hoc* order during the working day but, before they are processed, it may be necessary to sort the transactions into bookshop order or even book order. Although the resulting sorted file is still a transaction file, it is sometimes referred to as a *sort file*.

Backup files

In batch-processing systems, the transaction file is processed against the master file. With some file organisations, this master file update is achieved by copying the old version of the master file, record-by-record, on to a new master file whose records have been updated, where appropriate, by the transaction data. After this process, the transaction file and the old master file are still intact. They are not, however, discarded, since between them they can be used to create again the new master file if any corruption or damage occurs to it. The 'old' transaction and master files are said to be *backup files* and kept for security purposes. Figure 2.6 illustrates this idea.

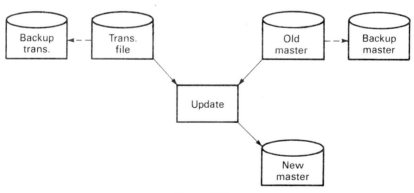

Figure 2.6

2.4.2 File organisation

There are a number of different ways in which a file can be organised and these depend on:

● the demands of the particular application
● the way in which the file is processed
● the storage media available

All storage media impose a physical sequence on the records stored in a file. This physical structure is very often incompatible with the logical view of the user and a way has to be found for mapping the logical requirements on to the physical structure. One important aspect to be considered in the design of the logical file organisation is the file activity. The most common statistic to be considered is the *hit rate*. This is defined as follows:

$$\text{Hit rate} = \frac{\text{No. of different records accessed}}{\text{Total number of records in the file}} \times 100$$

(it is often expressed as a percentage).

The organisations to be considered in this chapter are sequential, random, indexed sequential and list.

Sequential organisation

A sequential file is simply one with records sorted into a particular order depending on one or more of the fields (the key field(s)). The records are still stored in physically adjacent storage locations but they have some logical order. Thus a sequential file can be created by sorting a file. Figure 2.7 shows this process.

Sequential files can be accommodated on either magnetic tape or magnetic disc. To search for a particular record, all previous records have to be accessed although, if the file is stored on disc, the binary chop method of searching can be employed.[1]

Sequential organisation is particularly useful where an application demands a high hit rate. In a publisher's payroll system, for example, every record on the employee master file would need to be accessed and hence sequential organisation would be suitable. For low hit-rate applications, it would not be suitable.

With this type of organisation, insertion of new or deletion of old records can cause problems. For instance, if a new bookshop called DETTINGS opened an account, the record would have to be inserted between DENNYS and DILLONS. Although not impossible, it would be extremely difficult to shuffle all the records from DILLONS onwards up a space in order to make

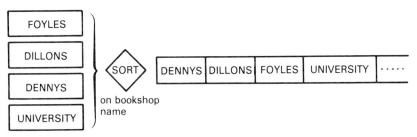

Figure 2.7

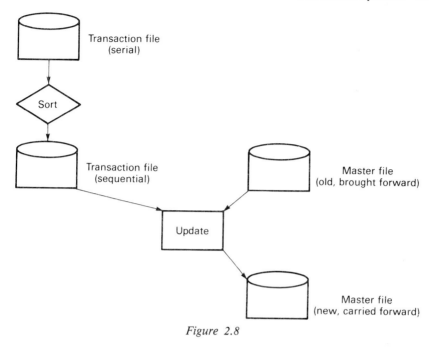

Figure 2.8

room for DETTINGS. Similarly, if FOYLES close their account, then deleting the record would leave a hole in the file and it is unlikely that another new bookshop could be conveniently squeezed in the correct sequence. Because of these problems, sequential files are always updated by copying, that is, taking an 'old' master file and producing a 'new' master file in the update run. This, as has already been explained, has the useful by-product of producing a backup master file. Furthermore, it follows that the most efficient processing can be achieved by sorting the transaction file into the same key sequence as the master file.

Figure 2.8 illustrates a typical batch-processing run for a sequential master file update.

Despite the disadvantages outlined above, sequential organisation is still a very popular method, especially for applications that require a large number of records to be updated during any particular computer run, for example, high hit rate such as payroll.

Random organisation

In a random file organisation, the physical order in which the records are stored bears no apparent relation to their local order. All direct-access storage media have directly addressable physical storage locations and these addresses are used to access individual records. So, unlike sequential organisations, a record on a random file can be accessed directly, regardless of whether or not previous records have been accessed. Random organisation is particularly useful for low hit-rate applications such as a typical enquiry system where one particular record needs to be accessed and displayed in order to answer a customer's query. Conversely, for high hit-rate applications, random file organisation is cumbersome and inefficient.

The addressable area on a magnetic disc is normally referred to as a *bucket* and, depending on the size of the records and the physical organisation of the disc, a number of records can be held in a bucket. The operation of a random file involves the storage in (and subsequent retrieval from) a particular unique bucket on the disc. Once the correct bucket is located, it can be searched until the desired record is found. It is therefore necessary to be able to associate a record with a particular bucket, and the record key field is used for this purpose. The key is used for both the initial storage and the subsequent retrieval of the record.

The way in which the relationship between the key and the bucket address can be established falls into three categories:

- directory look-up
- direct relation
- address generation

Directory look-up (sometimes referred to as 'dictionary') involves the setting up of a table which contains pairs of values, the key and the corresponding bucket address. When a particular record is required, a search is initiated for the appropriate key in the directory and, when it is located, its address is read. The address is then used to retrieve the desired record. This method is particularly efficient for small random files, but for larger files the directory may require special structuring, in the form of a tree, to enable fast searching.

Direct relation involves organising the records so that the key field corresponds to an actual bucket address. For example, a TYPESETTER record with TYPESETTER-ID = 17001 (the value of the key) would be stored in bucket number 17001. Space is allocated for each record regardless of whether it exists at the creation of the file. In this way the addition of new records during the life-cycle of the system is made easier.

Address generation is probably the most commonly used technique for the setting up and operation of a random file. Records are linked to a particular bucket by means of a *randomising* or *hashing* algorithm. The algorithm operates on the record key to generate a bucket address within the appropriate range on the disc. The key is not an address itself, merely a value used in order to calculate an address. Although a large number of different types of hashing algorithm exist, none of them are perfect in that when applied to two different keys, the same result (bucket address) may occur. This is the problem of synonyms: two different keys resulting in the same generated address.

This may not be too great a problem if each bucket can accommodate a number of records, since two synonyms can fit into the same bucket. However, it is often the case that a synonym cannot be accommodated in its 'proper' bucket and must be stored elsewhere. This can be handled in two ways:

(1) A synonym record can be stored in the next available bucket, and this is known as consecutive spill.
(2) A synonym record can be stored in a specially reserved area known as the file overflow area and the record is accessed by following a series of pointers. This is known as chaining or tagging.

If too many synonyms occur in a random file, accessing a particular record can be slow. Normally a record is located by a movement of the disc head to a particular track followed by a search of that track for the particular bucket. If a synonym has been displaced and the search is fruitless, the head will have to switch to the file overflow area and continue the search. The retrieval of a record is achieved by applying the same algorithm to the key as was used in the initial storage of the record.

To try and avoid problems of overflow, the buckets are never completely filled at file creation. New records will occur during the life of the system and will need to be fitted into their correct bucket. At creation, therefore, a packing density of the order of 50–60 per cent is often used. Suppose that each bucket can accommodate five logical records. When the file is created, a hashing algorithm is used which will result in most buckets containing three records, thereby leaving space for a further two. Such a file is said to have a packing density of $3 \div 5 \times 100 = 60\%$.

During the early part of the system life-cycle, the addition of new records is unlikely to cause problems, since on average there are two spare locations for each bucket. Subsequent access to these records is fast since most will be found in their home bucket. However, in a volatile application where many new records are continually added, there will come a time when the majority have to be placed in the overflow area. Subsequent access to these records will be much slower resulting in a degradation of the response time in retrieving a record: in short, the system slows down. Such a degradation is usually symptomatic of a random file becoming too full and, in order to regain the desired response time, the file has to be reorganised using a modified lasting algorithm.

There are very many different forms of hashing algorithm[1] and many of these are incorporated within system software and accessible via an application language such as COBOL or PL/1. All of them operate by applying some function to the record key, that is:

Address = f (key)

where f is discontinuous so that adjacent keys do not map on to adjacent bucket locations. One example of a hashing algorithm is known as *division taking remainder*. Two steps are involved in this technique, these being:

(1) Divide the record key by the number of available buckets and save the remainder.
(2) Add the start address for the file to this address.

Example: Records of 100 characters in length have their keys in the range 2000 to 5999. The file holds 3000 records and the bucket size is 512 characters. A packing density of 60 per cent is used and the file is to start from bucket 1000. The first requirement is to calculate the number of buckets required for the file. A bucket can potentially hold 5 records (512 ÷ 100) but, under a 60 per cent packing density, the file will be set up with 3 records per bucket. Therefore, 3000/3 = 1000 buckets are required and the address range for the file will be buckets 1000 to 1999.

The bucket address for a record is:

Address = (key mod 1000) + 1000

So for record with key 2524, the address will be:

(2524 mod 1000) + 1000
= 524 + 1000 = 1524

It is worth noting that synonyms will occur with this algorithm.

In designing a random file one has to consider certain factors that affect the processing of such a file. First, an appropriate algorithm must be chosen for relating the record key to a storage address. Second, overflowing and its effects must be considered at design time. At design time, the designer aims at minimising synonyms and, when the file is 'live', it is constructed in such a way as to minimise the *effect* of synonyms. The number of synonyms can be reduced by reducing the packing density, but this must be balanced against having too much unused space. In most cases, occurrence of synonyms is unavoidable. Their effect may be reduced by loading the most frequently accessed records first, forcing them to be stored at a home bucket. If the least accessed records are loaded last, although they have a high probability of being synonyms, their effect will not be as drastic since the required accesses to the overflow bucket will be kept to a minimum.

Indexed sequential organisation

This form of organisation is a compromise between sequential and random. For applications with a high hit rate, sequential processing (and hence file organisation) is the most efficient form of organisation, although this is inefficient for accessing one particular record from the file. On the other hand, low hit-rate enquiry-type systems are best served by random file organisation but this becomes inefficient if any sequential processing is required. Some applications may require both types of processing. For example, a payroll system with an enquiry suite (for individual employee's queries) would require sequential processing of all records for the production of payslips etc., but also fast access to individual records for dealing with employee queries. Such an application is a candidate for indexed sequential organisation.

An indexed sequential file is stored on a direct-access storage medium and consists of three distinct areas.

(1) *The index area.* This contains all the indices associated with the file.
(2) *The prime (or home) area.* This is the main storage area for the file's records.
(3) *The overflow area.* If this area exists, it will contain all displaced records.

The way an indexed sequential file is used resembles the ways a library user locates a book with the help of a card index. By consulting the index, the library user obtains a number that corresponds to the required book. Each row of shelves usually specifies the range of numbers of the books contained on them. Having obtained the book number, from the card index, the library user proceeds to the correct row by comparing this number to the displayed range of numbers in each row. Next, the shelves are searched sequentially until the required book is located.

In indexed sequential files, records are stored sequentially, but can be accessed directly by the use of indices. An index contains the key of a record together with its address. Not every record, however, has an entry in the index. Records are stored within tracks, and the address found in an index corresponds to a track number as opposed to an exact address. Also, in the index, only the key of the last record in a particular track, that is the record with the highest key within that track, is found. Indexed sequential files can only be supported on a direct-access device (magnetic disc). Figure 2.9 illustrates the idea of indices.

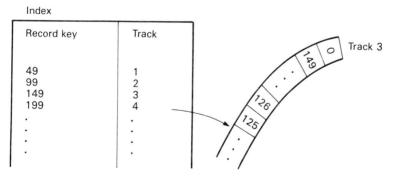

Figure 2.9

In most commercial applications the file would be large enough to occupy more than one *cylinder* of the disc pack. For such files, a two-level index is required. A primary (or cylinder) index identifies the highest key value on a particular cylinder. The heads then move to that particular cylinder where a secondary (or track) index is found. This indicates the highest key value on each track of that cylinder, and is usually stored on the first track of that cylinder.

When records are added to an indexed sequential file, overflowing is likely to occur. As with a sequential file, it is difficult to 'shuffle up' existing records to make space for the newcomer and so the new record can be placed 'out of sequence'. A number of tracks on each cylinder are normally reserved for overflows and are designated the cylinder overflow area. Since switching to the cylinder overflow area does not involve movement of the disc heads, a search of this area is therefore fast. Very often, cylinder overflow areas can become full and a second area, known as the file overflow area, is also reserved at the end of the entire file. Any record placed in the file overflow area, however, requires disc head movement to locate it, and this will slow the response time.

The insertion of new records can either be done by arranging them into the cylinder overflow area or, in many applications, by employing system software to rearrange the existing records on the track so as to accommodate the new ones. This rearrangement may result in displacement of the first record within the track and this will be stored in the overflow area. Deletion of records is usually achieved by marking such records as *logically deleted*. Actual physical deletion occurs when the file is 'cleaned up' periodically by running *housekeeping routines* from the system library. In addition to physical deletion of records, clearing the file also enables reorganisation of records and indices to remove records from the overflow areas and insert them in their correct sequence.

List organisation

The concept of the database is discussed fully later in this section. However, there is one type of file organisation which can be thought to bridge the gap between traditional file organisation and database: this is the list file organisation. A list simply means an ordered set of items, in this case records. A list file maintains a logical order of records by means of a series of pointers from each record to its logical successor. The important point, however, is that the logical ordering need bear no resemblance to the physical order; in other words, each record can be stored in any physical location as long as its predecessor 'knows' its address. So the pointers can be simply addresses of physical locations on the disc.

List file structures can vary in complexity from simple single pointer systems to complex multipointer. As an example, suppose a publisher

Head = 60

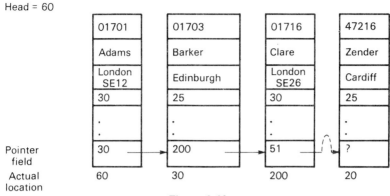

Pointer field

Actual location

Figure 2.10

wishes to store the author file as a simple list. Each author record occurrence would contain the relevant fields (code, name, address etc.) and, in addition, a field indicating the address of the 'next' author would be maintained. One further pointer, known as the head or the external access point, is maintained so that the first record can be accessed but thereafter each subsequent record is accessed via the pointer fields of its predecessor. Figure 2.10 illustrates the process.

The last record in the structure must contain a special symbol in the pointer field to identify it as the last one. This is shown in Figure 2.10 as a ?. Traversal of the list merely involves accessing each record, processing it, and then moving on to the next via the pointers. Records can be inserted anywhere in the list; any physical storage space can be used and, as long as the pointers are adjusted appropriately, the logical sequence is maintained. For example, if a new author (01710, Callan) were to be inserted in the Figure 2.10 structure, it could be physically located anywhere — in location 600, say. Then the pointer field for (01703, Barker) would become 600, that for (01710, Callan) would become 200 (pointing to 01716, Clare) and the logical sequence would be maintained.

Similarly, deletions are handled by realigning the pointers and then physically deleting the record. For example, the removal of Barker from Figure 2.10 would necessitate the pointer field for 01701 Adams becoming 200 so that it points to Clare, by-passing Barker which can then be deleted. There are a number of algorithms for the insertion and deletion of records in a list.

Sophisticated lists can involve extra fields for reverse pointing (each record holds the address of its logical predecessor) for circling (where the last record points back to the first) and for the setting up of inverted lists. An inverted list involves the setting up of one or more indices which are logically ordered by some other key and with each value of that key pointing to the appropriate record. Figure 2.11 shows an inverted list on author age.

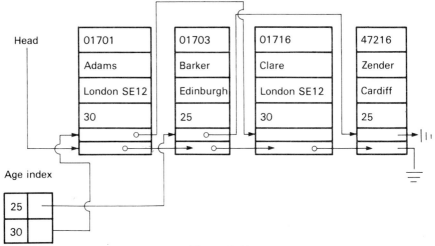

Figure 2.11

2.5 Database management systems

The list file structure described in Section 2.4.2 displayed flexibility in that the logical organisation was completely divorced from the physical organisation. The benefits of this resulted from the freedom of the application to insert new records in *any* available space without worrying about the logical structure being affected; as long as the pointers are maintained, the file functions effectively. In other words, the application software in a sense need not concern itself with how a record is physically stored, only with accessing a particular record. The natural progression from this concept is to remove the 'worry' about physical aspects of storage of data from *all* the application programs operating in an organisation. This concept of separating concern for the storage and retrieval of data from the actual processing of that data is the basis of a database system.

The difference between the database approach and the traditional file approach can be further explored by referring to Figures 2.12 and 2.13. If a publishing company operates a file-based information system, it may have three separate applications as shown in Figure 2.12.

These three application sub-systems provide valuable information, and each accesses a separate file. The author sub-system is concerned with the updating of details on the author file, the order sub-system processes orders from all the customers (bookshops) on a daily basis, the production sub-system is concerned with processing information for the production of new books, second editions, reprints etc. This is typical of file-processing environments where user requirements are treated in isolation in that the organisation of and access to the data files are separately determined for

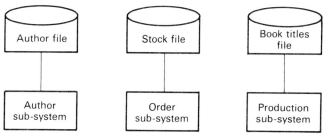

Figure 2.12

each application. Each set of data is associated with a particular application sub-system. In many information systems, however, it is necessary to have the ability to transcend these imposed barriers and access data right across the organisation. For example, suppose management wanted to know 'is it worth reprinting any of Clare's books?'

In the file-based environment this query would require data from all three sub-systems. First, in order to know the books written by Clare (and possibly other information about the author), it would be necessary to access the author sub-system. Secondly, to determine which of these books sell well, it would be necessary to access the order sub-system which will enable the interrogation of the stock file to determine the stock levels of Clare's books. Lastly, information on the production costs and time spans would be required and this is obtained from the production sub-system. Since the files in these sub-systems are likely to be of different organisation and the programs for access will be different, this type of query is not simple to answer.

In database environments, data for the whole organisation is viewed as

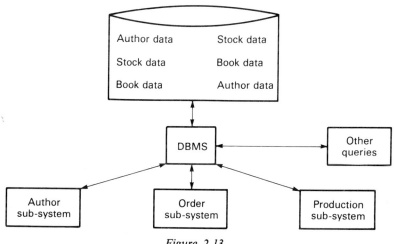

Figure 2.13

a whole irrespective of its type. No one individual, department or application system 'owns' its data; the philosophy is that any application from any part of the organisation can access the data that it needs. Since the mass of data in a database must be accessible by any application, its storage and retrieval must be carefully *managed* by a system 'outside' the normal application systems.

A Database Management System (DBMS) is the software that performs this task: the storage, retrieval and maintenance of the data. DBMS are general-purpose software packages developed and supplied by computer manufacturers. Figure 2.13 illustrates the approach for the publisher's information system.

The three application sub-systems are 'shielded' from the actual data by the DBMS.[1] Part of the DBMS provides each application with its own view of the data, and this view is matched with the requirements of the application; the view is totally different to the way in which the data is physically stored. Moreover, the DBMS also provides an interface to enable the *ad-hoc* enquiries (Is it worth reprinting any of Clare's books?) which proved so difficult in a file-based application.

2.5.1 The advantages of the database approach

The previous section illustrated some of the reasons why a database approach can be useful. There are a number of advantages of a database over a conventional file-based approach and the more significant of these are discussed in this section.

The reduction or elimination of redundancy

In file-based systems it is impossible to organise the data to suit all the applications—some will require sequential access, some random and some indexed sequential. Therefore, it is often the case that the same data has to appear in more than one file. For example, in the system illustrated in Figure 2.12, fields relating to book title occur in all three files. In such an environment, problems concerning the updating, inserting or deletion of data are likely to occur since this would have to be done in all three files. If this is not done, inconsistency will occur and one or more of the files will have incorrect data. The scale of the problem becomes greater the higher the number of files that are present. In a database environment, only one copy of the field is required and this can lead to savings in storage.

Integrity of data is maintained

Lack of data integrity can result from redundancy as outlined above. This means that the information generated by the data-processing system can no longer be trusted: the same data appearing in a number of files within a file-based system may not be consistent. In a database system, this problem is avoided because the data is only recorded once.

Independence of data is achieved

A database system relieves the applications programs of the responsibility for the organisation and physical storage of the data. In a file-based system, each program has this responsibility, and if two programs access the same file, both must contain definition of how the data in that file is organised. If the file needs to be restructured for any reason, then both the programs will have to be modified. This is avoided in a database environment since the physical structure of the data is invisible to the programs.

The sharing of data between applications is made easier

The sharing of data by different applications allows the users to gain valuable information by linking data across the organisation. Fourth-generation information systems are designed around departmental sub-systems accessing corporate data and integrating into a complete information system for the organisation. Data is not owned by individual departments but shared by all users. This is made much easier by employing a database system.

Central control of data

In database environments, the organisation and physical storage of data are divorced from the applications programs and controlled by the DBMS. This central control leads to better management of the data and this is vitally important because data is an important and valuable organisational resource. This control is normally exercised by a database administrator (DBA) who is responsible for the creation and maintenance of the database, liaising with the users at all times in order to identify their needs and deal with their problems. Among these responsibilities are:

- designing the database
- setting standards for data representation and documentation
- setting and administering rules about database usage
- selecting the most appropriate physical structure for the data and monitoring its efficiency
- monitoring all operations on the database

2.5.2 Database utilities and facilities

The successful creation and maintenance of a database depends very often on the availability of certain utilities that help the DBA to carry out his tasks in an efficient and reliable manner. These utilities form part of the software package that is purchased by the database buyer from the manufacturer or the software house. Some of these utilities are outlined below:

(1) *Data dictionaries.* These can be used both as development aids during the design and creation stages of a database and also, later, as maintenance aids. Data dictionaries include definitions of all the data types that are present in a database, thus providing one central source of information about data, from which analysts and programmers can work with a high degree of standardisation. When data dictionaries were first sold, most of them were offered by independent software houses. Nowadays, most database vendors offer their own data dictionaries which are able to interface with the resident database.

(2) *Report generators.* This is the name given to utilities that help produce printed reports and other specialised applications such as customised letters. Again, a simple command language is used for defining the parameters necessary for producing such reports. There have been claims in fact that the commands are so simple that casual users can start producing their own reports with just half a day's training. A user interacts with a report generator giving commands via a VDU. The report generator collects all the requested data from the database, forms a temporary file with those data and then, finally, prints this file according to some format specified by the user.

Report generators sometimes provide a facility for printing mock reports with any required format but with blanks instead of real data. When used in this mode, they can be very useful during the design stage of the application systems, by serving as communication aids between the designers and the system's users.

(3) *Query languages.* Most query languages are designed for non-specialists in data processing, and most of them are easy to learn and use. They are stand-alone 'languages' as their commands can be used outside any programs (which are written in a high-level language) and are very useful for *ad-hoc* requests. They are interactive English-like languages with usually simple unambiguous commands, making them ideal for casual users, who can obtain information from the database without having to know the logical or the physical organisation of the data.

(4) *Reorganising utilities.* These utilities help to reorganise the physical structure of the database, when the DBA decides that a more efficient organisation of the data is required.

(5) *Backup and recovery.* During the operation of a database system, data can be lost or damaged; therefore, some means must be provided by the DBMS for preserving its integrity. A typical approach is that of *journaling* where all transactions on the data, such as insertions, deletions and

modifications, are saved on a journal (sometimes called log) file. *Check-pointing* involves the saving of part of the database at certain points in time. If a failure occurs between two checkpoints, then by using the journal file the database can be reconstructed from the previous checkpoint.

(6) *Concurrency control.* Data in a database is shared by many users, usually accessing the data on-line, which means that it is possible for more than one user to access the same data occurrence. If two users attempt to modify the same data occurrence simultaneously, these actions will result in inconsistency. A DBMS can prevent the updates from overwriting each other by automatically locking the data that is modified.

A number of utilities have been discussed in this section. It is obvious that when a user decides to adopt or convert to a database system, this user does not purchase just another elaborate and clever access method to the organisational data, but a whole new environment, with the DBMS as its kernel and all the other utilities as its peripheral parts. These peripheral parts are very often essential for the successful development and maintenance of a database.

In addition to the utilities specified above which are used for the management of the data and for performing *ad-hoc* tasks, the DBMS must provide facilities for the use of database by applications programs requiring access to its data. These facilities can be categorised as definition, processing and maintenance of the data.

Data definition

The DBMS supports a *data definition facility* (DDF) which is used by the application programs to define the data that they require access to. The DDF is implemented via a data description language (DDL) which is used to define the relationships between the various pieces of data stored in the database. It is used to

- represent logical relationships determined by the data model (Chapter 7)
- name and describe all logical elements
- specify any security restrictions
- enable the DBMS to map the logical units of data to their physical storage structure

Two terms are commonly used in conjunction with data definition. A *schema* is a detailed description of all the record types and their associations in the database; it is the data definition or view of the entire database. Most applications, however, need to process just part of the data held in the

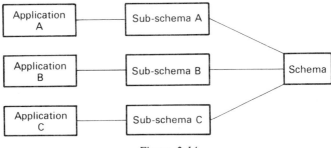

Figure 2.14

database. In other words, they require some sub-set of the schema for their own personal view. This sub-set is known as a *sub-schema* and each application program includes a copy of a specific sub-schema in order to define its access to the database. Figure 2.14 illustrates this relationship.

The schemas and sub-schemas will vary in syntax depending on the DBMS used, but typically would contain information on

● record name (author)
● field names (author code, author name ...)
● field descriptions (numeric, 5 digits, alphabetic, 30 chars ...)

Processing data

The application programs which make up the information system will be written in high-level languages such as COBOL or PL/1. Whereas in file-based environments, such programs would require full specification of data records and file organisations and definitions, in database environments these are replaced by the sub-schema. Additionally, the programs will contain statements that allow access to the data and these will be written in the DBMS data manipulation language (DML). Such statements are interpreted as calls to the DBMS. As with other statements in the program, the DML commands have to be checked for syntax and this is achieved by an extension to the host language compiler. The DML enables the programs to process data in a logical rather than a physical way by following the logical relationships stated in the sub-schema.

DMLs differ from one DBMS to another, but in most of them three primitive commands, control, retrieval and modification, will be found. Control commands are concerned with identifying which database the application program wishes to access, arranging buffers and other system resources and defining the kinds of operations that the program can use. Retrieval commands are concerned with identifying and accessing a set of data according to some selection criteria. Once the selected data has been retrieved, modification commands operate to update, delete or insert a subset of that data.

Maintenance of the data

The facilities of defining and processing data interact at execution time in order to maintain the database to reflect the current state of the organisation's business. This interaction is controlled by the database control system (DBCS) within the DBMS. The application program requires data and issues a DML command, at the same time referring to the sub-schema which contains the data relevant to the program. The DBCS co-ordinates this and interfaces with the operating system on the host computer in order to access the required data from disc. The data is transferred via system buffers to the user working storage area. The manipulation can then be done on the data by the application program.

2.5.3 Database organisation

The way in which the data is organised within a database can be categorised in three ways: hierarchical, network and relational. Each DBMS will use one of these methods as a basis for its operation and the following sections briefly describe the structures. For further study, a number of works are available.[2]

The hierarchical model

Relationships between attributes are expressed by considering record types and data items. Entity relationships are expressed as links between two record types. These relationships are viewed as parent—child relationships. In hierarchical structures, there is no need to actually name links since only one is permitted between any two record types. In every hierarchical structure there is one record type (the root) at the highest level and any number of dependent record types at lower levels. A parent is a record occurrence that has subordinate record occurrences called children, and each occurrence except for the root must be connected to a parent occurrence. Figure 2.15 illustrates the process.

All occurrences except for CATEGORY must be connected to a record occurrence at a higher level. In any database system there needs to be some means of inserting, deleting, retrieving and modifying record occurrences and these are undertaken by the DML. Hierarchical DMLs are classified according to the way they operate on the hierarchical definition tree and the common methods are tree traversal and hierarchical selection.

Tree traversal (as used by IBM's IMS) is a method whereby a tree structure is searched in a specified order, for example, postorder or inorder. The order can be physically represented as either sequential or direct (random) and these physical representations correspond to those specified under the traditional file organisations. The hierarchical structure and the

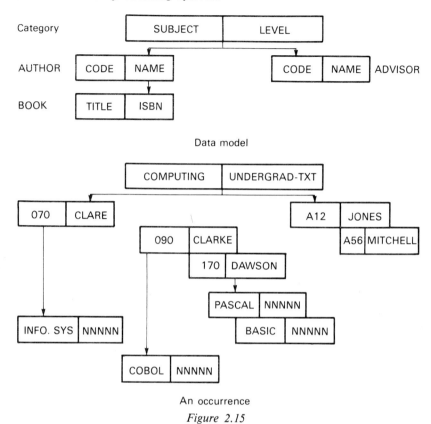

Data model

An occurrence

Figure 2.15

traversal mode determine the way in which record occurrences are inserted, retrieved or updated.

Hierarchical selection is a method where records are selected according to relationships between data items. Implementation is often in the form of an inverted list (Section 2.4.2) and basis retrieval commands such as PRINT and WHERE form part of the DML. For example:

PRINT AUTHOR-NAME WHERE TITLE EQ COBOL

would result in records satisfying the WHERE clause to be selected and the tree searched upwards to retrieve the appropriate author (Clarke).

The network model

Most DBMS implementing the network model follow the recommendations of the CODASYL report of 1971, together with subsequent enhancements. Chapter 7 describes different types of relationships between entities (1 : 1, 1 : n, n : n). Data analysis involves investigating and modifying these rela-

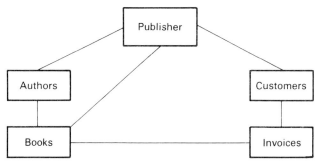

Figure 2.16

tionships and, if a model can be reduced such that the links between entities can be specified as 1 : n the resultant structure is known as a network structure.

Consider Figure 2.16. In a publishing company there may exist associations between entities specified in the figure. Most of these relationships are one to many (1 : n), for example, one customer will have a number of invoices, one author a number of books and so on. However, the relationship between books and invoices is n : m since one book can appear on a number of invoices and one invoice can relate to a number of books. This relationship can be transferred to 1 : n by introducing an entity Order which can act as a link between books and invoices ensuring all the resultant relationships in the structure at 1 : n. Figure 2.17 illustrates this.

Since there can be more than one link between entities, they should all be named. In linking records, a hierarchy is established between record

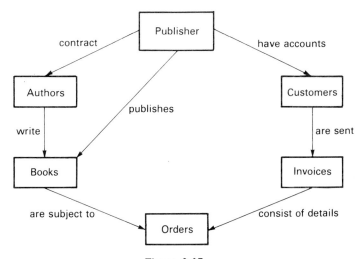

Figure 2.17

types by naming one as the *owner* and the other as the *member*, for example, Publisher is the owner and Author is the member in the contract relationship. This basis structure between record types is known as a *set type*. Using set types, the database designer can build a complete schema which consists of three basic points:

- data items
- record types
- set types

The set types provide logical links between record types and define the paths along which the system can locate the required data. A particular path for locating data about a particular order could be Publisher–Books–Orders or Publisher–Customers–Invoices–Orders. A record type may be an owner in one set type and a member in another or a record type may be a member in more than one set type.

Another consideration of the database administrator is that of membership class. Decisions need to be made on how member occurrences will be entered into the database (*the insertion mode*) and how they are subsequently manipulated (*retention mode*). The insertion mode may be *automatic*, where each occurrence of the member record type is automatically connected to its set. For example, each new invoice occurrence (automatic in 'are sent') must be assigned a customer on insertion. *Manual* mode is chosen when each occurrence of the member record type is specifically connected to the set by the application program using a DML command. Similarly with retention mode, *mandatory* membership means that occurrences of a record type cannot be removed from the occurrence of the set type once they have been connected — they can only be removed if they are completely deleted from the database. *Optional* membership is used where record occurrences are allowed to be moved from set occurrences by DML commands. These record occurrences will stay in the database as long as they appear in other set types.

The remaining issue to be addressed is that of mapping the set types on to the physical storage mechanisms.

When a record occurrence enters the database, the execution time component of the DBMS, called the database control system (DBCS), assigns a unique identifier to that record occurrence. This identifier is called a *database key*. Record occurrences are stored into blocks called *pages* whose size can be defined by the user. Each page has a unique number called a *page number* and within each page, each record occurrence is also given a unique number called a *line number*. The page number, together with the line number, provide a record occurrence with a unique location which is reflected in the database key. Pages are grouped together into larger subdivisions called *areas* (sometimes called *realms*). In a database there may be more than one area, and the number of areas is defined by the DBA in the schema definition. This physical organisation need not concern the user, as the actual 'placement' of each occurrence is transparent to him.

Nevertheless, the DBA has the choice — in the schema definition — of how record occurrences are to be organised and thus can obtain a variety of ways in retrieving them. The DBA can specify three *location modes*, called CALC, VIA SET and DIRECT.

(1) CALC. This is an abbreviation for calculation. When a record occurrence is stored in a page, the page is calculated by the DBCS from the value of one or more data items defined by the DBA in the schema. For example, the data item CUSTOMER-NO in the CUSTOMER record type may be used for calculating the database key if CALC is chosen. By choosing CALC mode, a record occurrence can be retrieved directly and a randomising algorithm spreads the record occurrences evenly over all the pages.

(2) VIA SET. When a record type is defined in the schema, the DBA can choose the VIA SET location mode, but this record type must be a member in a set type. The VIA SET mode is chosen so that a record occurrence is stored physically close to the other members of the set.

(3) DIRECT. This location mode permits the user to locate record occurrences in pages specified by him. It is not used as often as the other two modes.

The following example demonstrates the use of location modes.

Consider the record types CUSTOMER and ORDER and the set type 'are sent'. The DBA defines CUSTOMER with location mode CALC, using the data item CUSTOMER-NO as the symbolic key. ORDER is defined with location mode VIA are sent SET. Occurrences of CUSTOMER would be spread over a number of pages and any occurrence can be achieved directly through the symbolic key. Occurrences of ORDER are grouped together. These concepts are illustrated in Figure 2.18.

Because CUSTOMER is defined with CALC, 'Foyles' and 'Dennys' can be accessed directly, using the value of CUSTOMER-NO, and they are found in pages 099 and 1999 respectively. SUBJECT is defined with VIA SET mode and the occurrences 01, 02, 03 are grouped together in page 999 whereas 011 and 012 are located in page 1999.

A discussion on the physical representation would be incomplete without some mention as to how record occurrences are physically linked. A record occurrence can be thought of as consisting of two sections, its data and its pointers which relate that record occurrence to its NEXT, PRIOR or OWNER record occurrences. Figure 2.19 demonstrates record occurrences with NEXT pointers (a), with NEXT and PRIOR pointers (b) and with NEXT, PRIOR and OWNER pointers (c).

It should be emphasised that the application programmer never 'sees' these links which are implemented by the system. So far, only the data

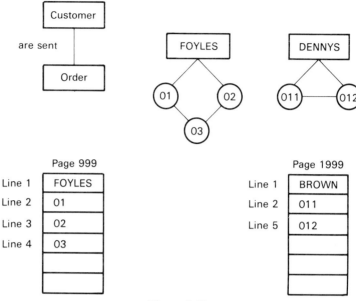

Figure 2.18

definition facility as defined by CODASYL has been considered. The other equally important function of a DBMS is the data manipulation facility. Rather than examining DML commands in detail, the reader is referred to the bibliography at the end of the chapter.

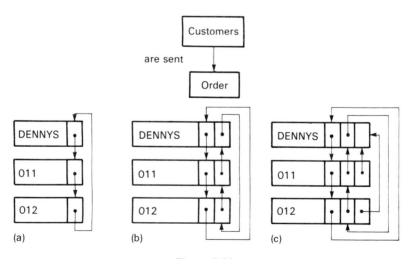

Figure 2.19

The relational model

Although the theoretical basis of the relational model has been in existence for over twenty years, being first investigated by E. F. Codd, it is only comparatively recently that DBMSs using this model have become available, ORACLE from Relational Software Inc., RAPPORT from Logica and IBM's SQL/OS are examples. Whereas hierarchical and network models use record types for representing attribute relationships and links for representing entity relationships, the relational model uses *relations* for expressing both types of connection.

A relation is best thought of as a table as illustrated in Figure 2.20. The RELATION customer has three columns called *attributes* and four rows called *tuples*; it is said to be of *degree* 3 and *cardinality* 4. The following properties hold:

(1) No two rows are identical
(2) The ordering of the rows is not significant
(3) The ordering of the columns is not significant

Values of attributes are extracted from areas of data called *domains*. Entity relationships are represented by data values extracted from the tables; all information is addressed by values in the tables and not by table position. However, the 'view' of data as tables is entirely a user view. Although they can be thought of as sequential files, they differ in that relational database systems support operations on entire tables whereas records in files are only operated on one at a time.

There are a number of different relations that can be set up on the same data and some have better properties in a changing environment than others. This concept is known as normalisation, that is the construction of appropriate records at analysis stage, and this topic is discussed in Chapter 7.

Associations can be represented by primary relations (existing ones) and it is possible to generate other relations from the primary relations. This is done by the use of *relational operators* acting on primary relations to generate *derived* relations. These relational operators can be described by *relational algebra* which consists of a set of operators that construct a required relation from existing (and intermediate) relations.

CUSTOMER	CUST-NO.	NAME	LOCATION
	123	FOYLES	LONDON
	176	DENNYS	LONDON
	184	CALLANS	LEEDS
	192	HARRISONS	MANCHESTER

Figure 2.20

BOOK

BOOK-NO	BOOK-TITLE	BOOK-AUTHOR
18191	DATA PROCESSING	LOUCOPOULOS
18272	DATA COMMUNICATIONS	CLARE
18844	PASCAL	OATEY
19664	COBOL	PAYNE
19875	ORGANISATIONS	SMITH

CUSTOMER

CUSTOMER-ID	CUSTOMER NAME	CUSTOMER-ADDRESS
123	FOYLES	LONDON
176	DENNYS	LONDON
184	CALLANS	LEEDS
192	HARRISONS	MANCHESTER

ORDER

CUSTOMER-ID	BOOK-NO	ORDER-DATE
176	18272	10.4.85
123	18191	16.9.85
184	18844	20.3.85
176	19875	30.8.85
123	18272	16.9.85

Figure 2.21

Referring to the publisher's example, suppose three relations exist; BOOK holds details of published books, CUSTOMER corresponds to bookshops who have accounts with the publisher and ORDER contains details about bookshops' orders for books.

BOOK   (BOOK-NO, BOOK-TITLE, BOOK-AUTHOR)

CUSTOMER   (CUSTOMER-ID, CUSTOMER-NAME, CUSTOMER-ADDRESS)

ORDER   (CUSTOMER-ID, BOOK-NO, ORDER-DATE)

The underlined attributes are the primary keys and the occurrences are shown in Figure 2.21.

The selection operator

Suppose that the publisher requires the name of CUSTOMER-ID 184. The selection operator can be used to specify this:

CUSTOMER (CUSTOMER = 184) =

which will result in:

CUSTOMER-ID CUSTOMER-NAME CUSTOMER-ADDRESS
184   CALLANS   LEEDS

This resultant relation has the *same* attributes as CUSTOMER but with only one tuple. This tuple does contain information about the ID and the address of the customer and this may not be of interest to the user. If the name only is required, then the *projection* operator should be used.

The projection operator

This is used to extract specified columns from a relation. Projection of ORDER over CUSTOMER-ID and BOOK-NO

ORDER (CUSTOMER-ID BOOK-NO) =

would give

176	18272
123	18191
184	18844
176	19875
123	18272

The join operator

It is possible to join two relations over a common domain. The result is a new relation containing all attributes from both relations. For example, if a user wants full details of outstanding orders, the query can be achieved by joining CUSTOMER and ORDER

CUSTOMER (CUSTOMER-ID = CUSTOMER-ID)ORDER =

to give

CUSTOMER-ID	CUSTOMER-NAME	CUSTOMER-ADDRESS	BOOK-NO	ORDER-DATE
123	FOYLES	LONDON	18191	16.9.85
123	FOYLES	LONDON	18272	16.9.85
176	DENNYS	LONDON	18272	10.4.85
176	DENNYS	LONDON	18975	30.8.85
184	CALLANS	LEEDS	18844	20.3.85

The division operator

This is where a binary relation is divided over a common domain to provide a table of attributes satisfying the operation. For example, suppose we were interested in certain orders made on specified dates, that is:

SPEC-DATES	ORDER-DATE	REV-ORD	CUSTOMER -NO	ORDER -DATE
	10.4.85			
	30.8.85		176	10.4.85
			123	16.9.85
			184	20.3.85
			176	30.8.85
			123	16.9.85

Then:

REV-ORD (ORDER-DATE − ORDER-DATE) SPEC-DATES

would give

CUSTOMER-ID
176

Both hierarchical and network systems are constrained by their format. A user has to be aware of the *access path* between record types (tree traversal in hierarchical models and set types in network models). In relational models, relationships can be defined or derived by constructing new relations from existing ones. These models can be thought of as black boxes that are able to service any user demand. Despite this 'black box' approach though, access paths still exist in relational models. The joining of the two relations CUSTOMER and ORDER (in the example) can be implemented in a number of ways, such as using pointers or creating a new relation file. This, however, is all transparent to the user who does not need to know how the join is to be implemented in order to demand this operation from the system.

The mapping of relations to physical storage is possibly the single hardest obstacle in the implementation of relational systems for large volumes of data. The problem arises because of the need for inter-file communication and fast searching mechanisms, which most hardware architectures do not handle efficiently. A possible solution to this problem is the introduction of special hardware architecture for supporting relational DBMSs. In such a system, most of the searching and retrieving between relations is achieved by the hardware.

It is widely accepted that for large volumes of data, special hardware may be needed for handling relational databases. In this way the hardware is designed around the software rather than the other way round as has been the tradition since the early days of computer development. A low-cost 'database processor' has been designed and is commercially available, for running relational databases. The intelligent database machine (IDM), as it is called, can be used as a stand-alone data-management device or as a back-end machine supporting a mainframe or a mini-computer. Data is held on disc and is retrieved by special-purpose hardware which is much faster than using software to carry out the same operations. The designers claim a data-transfer rate of 20 Mbytes per second. The IDM can manage up to 50 databases, each one having 32 000 relations and each tuple having up to 2000 bytes. Any relational data language can be used and, at present, INGRES has been chosen as the query language.

2.6 Summary

The last decade has seen a dramatic increase in the number of users that employ DBMSs to solve and support their information needs. This has come about because of the difficulties and operational inefficiencies that are presented by many file-processing systems. Data is often locked in files, accessed only by specific programs that know the structure and organisation of the files concerned. As information systems invariably grow, so does the complexity and cross-referencing of files and programs that operate on them. The result at the end may be a complex monolithic and inefficient data-processing system. The main requirement from a DP system is the provision of information so that humans can make decisions. If this information is inaccurate or out-of-date, then it is of little use. DBMSs provide some means of easy access to data, efficient management and relatively easy system growth.

2.7 References

1. Clare, C. P. and Loucopoulos, P. (1986). *Data Processing: current theories and practice*, 2nd edn, Abacus Press.
2. Date, C. J. (1975). *An Introduction to Database Systems*, Addison Wesley.
3. Martin, J. (1975). *Computer Database Organisation*, Prentice-Hall.
4. Hanson, O. 'Basic File Design', *Computer Weekly Handbook*.
5. Deen, S. (1977). *Fundamentals of Database Systems*, Macmillan.
6. Champine (1980). *Distributed Computer Systems*, North Holland.

CHAPTER 3
Office systems

3.1 Introduction

Commercial organisations have always been among the first to make use of new technology. This is because their very environment insists on exploitation of every advantage in the battle to be competitive, cost-effective and attractive to employees. Apart from the computerisation of information systems discussed in Chapter 1, the most notable early use of automation in the commercial world was the use of computer-controlled machinery, either to replace or to assist workers in various tasks. Computer-aided design (CAD) and computer-aided manufacture (CAM) have had a great impact on a number of industries with, for example:

(1) Robotics, where computer-controlled machinery has become an efficient alternative to man, particularly in repetitive, intricate and dangerous tasks (CAM).
(2) Technical drawing, where an engineer may use a computer to model reality and layout drawings, using the computer to produce detailed drawings as required (CAD).

More recently, with advances in micro technology, software has been developed to create systems for the office environment. Just as CAD/CAM systems have assisted the manual and technical sections of industry, similar systems are becoming the tools of the office worker. A great deal of money is spent on staff to give general office support and any improvements in cost-effectiveness in this area would obviously be welcome.

The majority of tasks facing the office worker involve the manipulation of information, by collecting, creating, distributing and sorting of data. The traditional medium for registering data is, of course, paper. Manipulation of information on paper is costly, time-consuming and inefficient. An automated system for the office environment can assist the office worker in many of his tasks by providing facilities such as:

(1) *Filing.* Automated filing and ordering of data by the computer on the systems storage medium. Stored data is thus easily accessed for reference or use; no more inefficient, bulky filing cabinets.

(2) *Data processing.* Rapid calculations performed on stored and new data, results being presented in a variety of formats, as required, for example pie charts, histograms, tables. Many other types of calculations are also available, using stored data such as future trend predictions.

(3) *Document processing.* The word processor, the ability to type documents into the system, store them for future reference, correction, updating or merging, with other stored text, and print when required.

Many of the tasks performed by the automated office system are limited, almost solely, by the imagination and ability of the software designer.

An office worker does not, however, exist in a business vacuum. It would be extremely unproductive and inefficient for each individual to have his own automated filing system. A great deal of data 'owned' by an organisation is used by a number of different departments, and data created by one worker may be needed by another; similarly, documents prepared in one department may well be intended for other departments to incorporate within documents that they have prepared.

The systems must, therefore, be organised in such a manner that within the one organisation there is global access to all of the data files, although access to some data can, of course, be limited if required for security purposes. In this way, data may be maintained in one central store and readily used by those who need it. Each individual will have all necessary information at his fingertips without the despatch of any paper or the time and cost that would have been involved.

3.2 Inter-office communication

Apart from face-to-face meetings, inter-office communication can take two forms — telephone conversations and memos. These methods of communicating use what are, perhaps, the original office automation tools — the typewriter and the telephone. The word processor has already been discussed as an alternative to the typewriter in document processing. However, the automated office can offer one tool with which to replace the memo and also act as an alternative to the inter-office telephone call and this is the electronic mail system (EMS).

3.2.1 The telephone

In 1980, Butler, Cox and Partners Ltd produced figures demonstrating the numbers of various types of office communicating equipment, installed in UK offices, per thousand of working UK population. These are detailed in Figure 3.1.

The predominance of telephones in this list emphasises the importance placed upon that instrument as a means of communication and also the real need for people to have a reliable, real-time means of contact. However, using the telephone, as a means of contact in order to collect or give information, has a number of drawbacks which can be both time-consuming and frustrating, neither of which is conducive to an ideal working environment.

Problems encountered when using the telephone as a means of communication include:

(1) Telephone 'tag', the name given to the, not infrequent, problem of catching the intended recipient of your call at, or near, a phone. Research in the USA has shown that only 28 per cent of office-to-office telephone calls contact the required person at the first try.
(2) Ringing telephones need to be answered, possibly interrupting meetings or creative thought.
(3) Due to the interactive requirements of a telephone conversation, answers may not be fully considered.
(4) The required person may be away from his office for either a short time or a longer period.
(5) Telephone calls are normally restricted to one recipient, resulting in a number of calls to convey the same message to all those concerned.
(6) In an automated office, the information to be discussed may not yet have arrived with the recipient of the call.
(7) Telephone conversations are rarely recorded.

Communicating device	No./1000
Telephones	400
Data terminals	7
Telex terminals	4
Facsimile terminals	2
Communicating word processors	1

Figure   3.1

3.2.2 The electronic mail system

The electronic mail system (EMS) provides an attractive alternative to the telephone call, and is not affected by the problems listed above. 'Calls' are made using a terminal, workstation or similar device and messages typed at the connected keyboard. The sender may select any number of linked devices at which the text will then appear. Of course, restricted messages are accessible only at the intended station. Thus EMS can be seen to offer a number of advantages:

(1) Messages may be registered as urgent and/or requiring a reply.
(2) Recipients of calls may reply when convenient and, if necessary, after time for thought.
(3) Calls need not interrupt; messages may be read when the recipient is ready.
(4) Mail will be waiting for the recipient when he returns to his office, since calls do not get 'lost'.
(5) Any number of selected stations may receive a message and, using this method of communication, the memo can also be replaced by EMS.
(6) Persons absent from their offices, but still within the establishment, may be contacted by sending messages to all stations. This can be thought of as a form of 'paging'.
(7) Messages sent back and forth, as a conversation, are automatically recorded and may be stored for future reference.

It can be seen that the phone call can often be replaced by the use of urgent mail, and the memo by non-urgent broadcast electronic mail.

3.2.3 Software in the automated office

An electronic mail system is often thought of as the mainstay of an automated office system. To run an effective EMS, each office worker must have access to a workstation (microcomputer) which is linked to a network connecting other workstations. User-friendly software to manage the mail system must be provided to operate on an appropriate local area network (aspects of networking are discussed in Section 3.3). There are, however, other pieces of software which are necessary in order to accommodate the tasks of the office worker and these are listed below.

Word processing

In many organisations, a great deal of traditional document production is centralised in a typing pool. If this were also the case in the automated office, a copy of the appropriate software could reside on the office computer of the typing pool and be accessed by the workstations in that office. Alternatively, a copy could be stored on the individual workstation storage units, if there is sufficient capacity. If word processing were a minor part of the requirements of the office, the package could be stored on and accessed from just one computer in the network.

Storage and retrieval of information/data

Different levels of storage can be identified ranging from the corporate storage of information which needs to be kept permanently and be accessible by all members of the organisation, to the short-term personal storage of the individual office worker. Intermediate levels may also be necessary for security reasons, for example office-only storage or desk-only storage. How these are implemented is, of course, dependent on the hardware available, but the task is common to all levels: to retrieve a file (document) from store and display, print or send it to another workstation.

With appropriate levels of protection from unauthorised access, all the levels of information storage and retrieval could be operated from the organisation computer and disc files. A more attractive solution, however, would be to distribute the information storage and retrieval throughout the network so that, for example, information is stored on the disc of the workstation to which it has been sent. The bulk of the software would still be stored and run on the organisational computer but would access the appropriate information stored on discs in other parts of the network.

Data processing

A two-fold requirement exists: to develop and run programs or access packages on computers local to the network and to be able to interact, if necessary, with the corporate data-processing systems of the organisation. The former is fairly straightforward assuming that the workstations have sufficient power and capacity. Instead of executing commands, relating to running the automated office software, normal editing and operating system facilities of the microcomputer system are used. When interacting with the corporate data-processing systems, the workstation needs to appear to the DP computers as an 'ordinary' terminal. A certain amount of message switching and possibly data conversation will have to be undertaken by the office automation software to accommodate this requirement.

Links with other systems

Part of the software must be capable of undertaking the data conversion tasks which may be necessary when the automated office is linked with another organisation.

3.3 Local area networks

In order to link the various workstations for the purpose of distributing data and, more importantly, to provide an EMS, a transmission system is required which will allow interactive use. That is, the system must give high

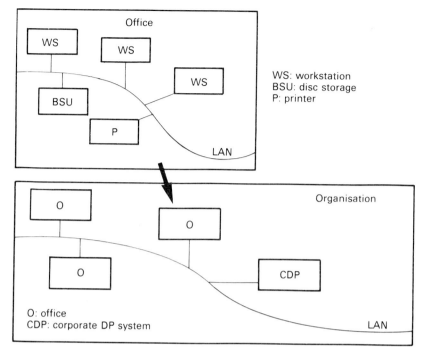

Figure 3.2

transmission rates, fast response times and a low error rate. It must also link various devices, including intelligent workstations, storage units and printers, in order that mail may be 'stored and forwarded' if necessary. All the requirements for the successful linking of remote office devices are catered for by the use of a local area network (LAN). Figure 3.2 illustrates this.

3.3.1 Development of LANs

The groundwork for LANs was formed in the 1960s in the search for new telephone technology. These developments were limited by the cost and lack of reliability of the available electronics. The idea of common digital communications systems was further developed, in the 1970s, by a number of research laboratories, and the variety in research and development led, largely, to the types of LAN commercially available today. However, the various approaches to LANs, in general, produce the same attributes:

● inexpensive transmission media
● inexpensive devices to interface to these media
● easy connection to the media
● high data transmission rates

- network data transmission rates independent of rates used by attached devices
- every attached device having the potential to communicate with every other attached device
- in the majority of cases, each device hears (but does not necessarily process) data intended for all other devices, as well as itself.

It should be noted that the data transmission rate, the method of attachment and the topology of the network are not important although, as will be seen, the transmission rate figures highly in the attempts at defining a LAN.

3.3.2 Defining a LAN

'In its simplest form, a LAN consists of a physical medium (typically an electronic cable) linking a set of user stations which themselves contain sufficient logic and electronic circuits to enable them to use a network.'[1]

'A LAN is a communications system that carries one or more digital channels round a building or other facility in such a manner that many devices may obtain brief exclusive use of the channel from time to time.'[2]

The definitions given above refer mainly to the facilities offered by a LAN, and the majority of attempts at a definition rely more on the physical attributes of the system to separate a LAN from other communications systems. Thurber and Freeman claim that theirs has been the only in-depth attempt to develop a universally acceptable definition of a LAN. They have also identified many parameters on which LAN definitions have been based. Thurber and Freeman propose three criteria to define a LAN:[3]

- single organisation ownership
- distances involved to be within a few miles
- use of some type of switching technology

Others such as Metcalfe and Boggs[4] describe LANs by relating them to the extremes of networking — 'near the middle of this spectrum is the LAN, the interconnection of computers, to gain the resource sharing of computer networking and the parallelism of multiprocessing' — and fitting them into their networking spectrum as shown in Figure 3.3.

It is obvious that there is, as yet, no universally accepted set of criteria, let alone values for these criteria, for defining a LAN. The most common standard would appear to be geographical scope, with transmission rate a popular second. However, it is unclear why some authors have included certain criteria in their definitions. The physical attributes of a LAN, which one would expect a definition to describe (situated in a single block of offices), will not change simply because of dual, or even multi, ownership.

Activity	Separation (km)	Bit rate (Mbps)
Remote	>10	<0.1
LAN	0.1–10	0.1–10
Multiprocessors	<0.1	>0.1

Figure 3.3

Even transmission rates may be considered as redundant as accurate specifiers of a LAN, since as technologies and research advances, systems, which are unquestionably accepted as LANs, are achieving rates far in excess of any specified in the definitions.

The most important criterion in the standardisation of LANs is the distance that they encompass. This area, as many definitions show, seems to be the all-important feature which distinguishes the LAN from other types of network such as wide area networks and computer buses. Rather than specify an area in mathematical terms, perhaps the boundaries of a LAN should be expressed as being within one establishment, building or set of buildings. The definition presented by Gee[1] would, with additional limits, appear to be the most practical and acceptable categorisation of a LAN: 'A physical medium, for example cable, coax, optical fibre, linking a set of user stations, each with logic and intelligent circuits to enable them to use the network. The stations being contained within a restricted area, for example office block, set of buildings; without the use of any public medium.'

There are a number of different systems of LAN commercially available and so, regardless of theoretical definitions and actual requirements, a practical model must abide closely to the specifications offered by these. Naturally the commercially available LANs have a number of fundamental differences, each giving advantages and disadvantages with respect to speed, errors, cost etc. However, as will be demonstrated, the primary identifiable difference is their topology.

3.3.3 Network topology

There are a number of possible topologies to be used in implementing LANs. Some of these can be seen to be developments of traditional computer linking methodologies, others can be specifically attributed to research programmes. In fact, research carried out at different centres can be directly related to the differing commercial attitudes regarding the leading LAN topologies which are available today.

Star

Star networks, traditionally used in many large computer sites, use a central switch to connect a number of devices, as shown in Figure 3.4. Each device has its own line with the switch effectively joining two devices together. In theory, this is not a LAN because the switch, not the medium, is the common factor to all nodes. These networks normally work in polled mode, the switch giving control to any node that requests it, either until that node is finished or the switch decides to give control to another. Although addition of new nodes to a star network is easy (simply plug a new line into the switch), in practice the new cable must be laid from the switch to the required node. Apart from the cost of supplying individual cabling, the switch must also possess a port for each node on the network.

Complex networks can be set up by interconnection of star systems; however, the cost of extensive cabling together with the problems of installing new lines make the star network less attractive in the office environment.

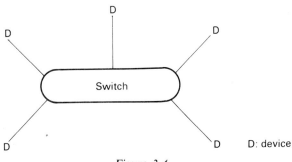

Figure 3.4

Tree

The tree network can be considered as a number of connected star systems as illustrated in Figure 3.5. As such, it suffers from the disadvantages that affect the star, such as the expense of individual lines for each node and the reliance of the network on the switch for successful transmission (if the switch goes down, the whole system is disabled).

Loop

Devices connected by loops have a common medium but one device controls all others on the loop. Traditionally, loops have been used to connect devices by low-speed lines. Loops have been likened to both ring and bus networks — a ring with one control node or a bus with both ends joined. These comparisons illustrate the disadvantages of the loop, which consequently is not often used in the LAN technology.

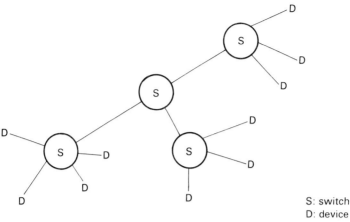

S: switch
D: device

Figure 3.5

Mesh

The mesh or fully/semi-interconnected network is largely used in networking distant nodes, where the environment around the transmission may be difficult (necessitating alternative routes between nodes) and where transmission routes need to be optimised in order to minimise costs (see Figure 3.6). The connection of many nodes or, in the case of a fully interconnected mesh, the connection of each node to every other, is not normally used in a LAN, except in situations where real-time response is imperative, such as in process control installations. In a LAN where the environment is more favourable, transmission bandwidth is not so restrictive and reliability is not so important, the complex logic for optimising routes and the great increase in cable costs are an unnecessary expense.

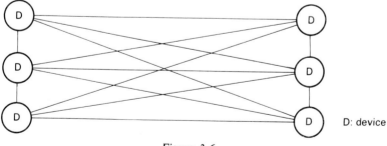

D: device

Figure 3.6

Ring

The ring network takes its name from the topology of the system — the transmission medium forms a ring, with a number of nodes connected.

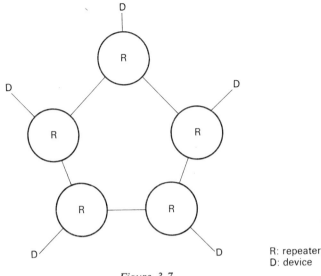

R: repeater
D: device

Figure 3.7

Each node is connected to the nodes on either side and no other. Transmission of data is usually unidirectional with each node's receiver receiving data on one side and, if that data is not for that node, retransmitting it to the next in the ring. The receiver is powered either by the attached device or by the ring itself (Figure 3.7).

There has been some criticism of the ring network as each node must be operative in order that data may be circulated around the ring. In order to overcome this possible unreliability, a number of variations on the original design have been developed:

(1) *Star-shaped ring.* Each node on the ring is at the apex of a star's fingers, the loops of cable before and after each node passing through a common 'wire centre'. This wire centre, passive in normal operation, has the ability to isolate one finger of the star should a node become faulty. This reliability is expensive, as the amount of cable used is far in excess of the amount necessary for a ring of normal topology to cover the same area.

(2) *Duplicate ring.* In this case, should the transmission medium be broken, an alternate ring can be used. This duplicate ring would normally be installed at the time of the original. Although this method of security gives some protection, any physical damage such as the collapse of ducting or severance by maintenance work may well affect both rings, as the same routing will most probably have been used for both cables. This drawback will also apply to a variation of the duplicate ring, which supplies an alternative route between each node without providing a complete duplication of the transmission ring.

(3) *Bypass ring.* Here a node has connections to nodes other than those immediately adjacent to it (while normal links to these are still maintained). If a break occurs in the medium, or a node goes down, an alternative route is available that will omit the broken section/node. The obvious drawback is the isolation of a working node due to the malfunctioning of an adjacent section of cable.

(4) *Reverse routing ring.* If this system suffers a break in its transmission medium, the nodes adjacent to the broken section will retransmit data back in the direction from which it came. That is, each node will both receive and transmit data from and to both directions. The two nodes that become the 'ends' of the ring 'close' up the ends and recirculate all data that arrives.

While the above variations improve the reliability of the ring and are, in fact, used by a variety of manufacturers, it must be pointed out that the added expense of cable, more complex repeaters and software to control the reconfigurations (necessary with some of the above styles) may well outweigh the need for such security in the office environment.

Bus

The bus network is simply a development of the data bus, used in computer systems, for the connection of processor, memory and peripherals. As in a computer system, all devices on a bus LAN are connected to a common transmission medium and share its use (Figure 3.8).

Unlike the ring networks, the data bus is completely passive. Every node must listen, in order that any data intended for a station will not be missed.

As already mentioned in the discussion of other topologies, the network is vulnerable to physical damage. While it is possible that a break in the transmission medium may give rise to two, non-connected, functioning buses, it is more probable that none of the bus will be usable. Again a duplicate medium may well be installed; however, as this is most likely to be routed with the original, any physical damage would probably affect both.

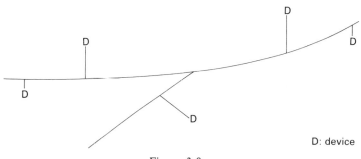

Figure 3.8

3.3.4 Transmission techniques

There are even more transmission techniques than there are topologies for LANs. Each topology may be combined with some or all of these techniques, giving an awesome number of possible basic networking systems.

However, since detailed discussion of transmission data is beyond the scope of this book, only a brief description is given of those combinations of topology and transmission techniques which are most popular in the commercial world today. This popularity stems partially from the influence of the manufacturers on the prospective purchasers and also the influence that the manufacturers can bring to bear on the various standards committees.

The most recent (1982) set of standards to be developed are those proposed by the IEEE 802 Traffic Handling Committee:

● the token passing ring
● the contention bus

and in the UK, although not considered by the IEEE 802 Committee, the accepted, unofficial British standard:

● the slotted ring

The contention bus and the slotted ring are the most widely used methods of implementing LANs, the bus in the USA and the ring in the UK. As yet the token passing ring is little used, although once IBM have finalised their experimental version of this system there will, no doubt, be a change in the balance of use. However, as the token passing ring can physically be considered in the same manner as a slotted ring, by reviewing the Ethernet and the Cambridge ring as examples of the contention bus and slotted ring respectively, the majority of commercially available LANs will be covered. As mentioned above, there are a number of systems which, in order to provide security and reliability, are rather more complex, but their basic designs may be considered as covered by the simple examples which follow.

Ethernet

The contention bus system as used by Ethernet can be seen as a development of the technique implemented by the ALOHA systems, a radio network in Hawaii. ALOHA terminals transmitted at any time, using a checksum in the data to ensure that only correct data was accepted. Due to the number of collisions, caused by this indiscriminate signalling, throughput was only around 19 per cent of the total network potential.

The Ethernet mimics the transmission of signals across the 'ether' by using a coaxial cable as a medium. The topology is that of an unrooted tree, so only one path may exist between stations to ensure correct sequencing of signals. The transmission medium is made up of 500 m lengths of cable, to which a maximum of around 100 stations can be comfortably attached. Repeaters allow any number of these cable segments to be connected, as long as any one route is a maximum of 1500 m and contains no more than two repeaters and nodes. The extremes of the system must not exceed a separation of 2700 m. Also included may be one point-to-point cable of a maximum 1000 m. Such a maximum Ethernet allows for the attachment of 1024 nodes.

The real success of Ethernet can be attributed not to the medium nor the topology but to the improvement on the original ALOHA use of the 'ether' as a transmission medium. All of the nodes attached to the system listen continuously for signals intended for them and they may also transmit signals at any time. With a possible 1024 attached stations on a system, this could obviously cause chaos should all of them wish to transmit at the same time. (The Ethernet message packet actually has the capability to address an enormous number of stations — allowing for interconnection of networks in the future.) To overcome the problem of collisions reducing the number of successful transmissions, the designers of Ethernet have used the carrier sense multiple access with collision detection (CSMA/CD) technique. Basically, CSMA/CD ensures that each station will listen while transmitting then, if any other transmissions are received while that station is still transmitting, it will know that a collision has taken place. If a collision occurs, both stations will not retransmit until a randomly set time interval has elapsed. This random time interval is a multiple of 51.3 ms. If on subsequent tries another collision occurs, the time interval increases exponentially, up to a maximum of 65 ms after ten tries. This interval then remains constant for another five attempts. On the failure of the 16th transmission, the attempt is abandoned and the monitor station informed (this situation would normally occur only with a breakage in the coaxial cabling).

In order that the CSMA/CD technique may be successful, the packet size must be matched to the physical separation of stations on the system. That is, in the worst case, a station will be just finishing one transmission when it receives the first part of a transmission from another station. This optimum size for an Ethernet message packet, on a network of the maximum size, is 576 bits. Obviously an Ethernet with only one segment of 500 m could use a smaller packet, if required, but as most of the delay in packet speed is due to encoding, decoding, repeaters, tranceivers etc., and not the coaxial cable, the optimum packet would only be reduced by 104 bits. Thus the 576 bit packet is normally adhered to for all Ethernets.

The use of CSMA/CD has meant that 90 per cent of signals are completed successfully. However, it must be pointed out that as use of the system increases, the success of immediate transmission decreases.

The Ethernet supplies a robust network but:

- packet delivery is not guaranteed but performed on a 'best effort' basis
- response time cannot be guaranteed; there is always the possibility of a delay
- packet size must always relate to the size of the network, making upgrading of the speed of the system extremely difficult.

The Cambridge ring

The Cambridge ring network is the direct descendant of telephone research. The idea for the original development arising from a visit made, by Professor Wilkes of the University of Cambridge, to the Swiss telecommunication company Hasler, where an experimental ring had been developed to carry digitised speech.

The transmission medium used for the Cambridge ring is two pairs of unshielded twisted wires. Nodes are connected to the ring by ring stations, or repeaters. These repeaters are powered by 50 V d.c. carried on the cable. By powering the repeaters from the ring, integrity is aided and the attached devices need not be switched on, or even functional. The purpose of the repeater is to regenerate any signals received and transmit them to the next node in the ring. All nodes are treated identically, except for the monitor and the logging stations. The monitor initialises the ring and maintains the integrity of the slots used for signalling. The logging station is responsible for recording errors.

In theory the signalling system will allow transmission of up to 300 m, and distances of around 200 m have been proven. However, repeaters are normally situated a maximum of 100 m apart, not because of signal attenuation, as it is often believed, but in order that any small percentage difference in the length of the four cables, used as the transmission medium, does not cause a slight difference in propagation time between repeaters, allowing signals to become out of phase. Meticulous matching of cables will allow greater distances between repeaters, but this is not generally worth the effort and cost involved.

As in the Ethernet system, the most important feature of this network is the method of data transmission. Although the original ring, developed at the University of Cambridge, used the register insertion method of transmission, this was soon replaced by the present technique, the empty slot. The register insertion method involves switching a register, or buffer, into the ring when sending a message packet; the register stays in series with the ring until the return of the packet, when it is removed. The basic problems in the use of this method were found to be maintenance and reliability. The switching circuits used in controlling the register must be fast enough to add, and then remove, the register from the ring without the loss of any bits. Any malfunction in the switches might cause a register to remain in the ring, resulting in a degrading of the whole ring.

The empty slot signalling technique is based on the idea of one, or more, empty packets circulating around the ring. A node with data to send waits for an empty packet, enters its data, the destination address, and its own address and sets the in-use flag. This packet then continues around the ring, being passed from node to node, until it arrives at the intended destination. The receiving node extracts the data, sets a marker to indicate that the packet has been read, and passes the packet on to the next node in the ring. The used packet thus arrives back at the originating node, which recognises it as the one sent out, resets the in-use flag and the packet is available for use by the next node that requires it. The packet cannot be reused immediately by the node that has just used it for transmission, but must be passed on around the ring, ensuring that one node with a large amount of data to transmit cannot 'hog' the ring. If the same packet circulates the ring and returns unused, the node is then allowed to reuse it.

The monitor station sets a flag in the packet as it passes, thus if a packet passes the monitor more than once, without being read or reset, it is obviously an error, can be recognised as such, emptied by the monitor and an error logged. Each packet consists of 38 bits, 8 of these being used for the address field giving 254 possible destinations for data, the monitor is address 0 and address 255 is used as a 'broadcast' mode. Interestingly, some versions of Ethernet networks use the slotted technique in order to improve transmission rates when the system is under heavy load. When a large number of collisions have occurred, the channel is allocated, to the users, on a slotted basis, so avoiding further collisions.

As with the Ethernet system, the physical size of the medium can affect the signalling technique. In the Cambridge ring, the number of circulating slots may be restricted by the size of the ring. The Cambridge ring presently operates at around 10 Mbps. However, experiments have been conducted on a larger ring with bigger slots with speeds up to 100 Mbps. Although 10 Mbps is the operating speed of the ring, 60 per cent of the bandwidth is taken up by control digits and so the available capacity for data is 4 Mbps. Also, as any node can only use one packet on the ring at any one time, the rate is further reduced and depends on the number of packets on the ring. The capacity available to any one node, where there are n packets on the ring, is approximately $4/(n + 2)$ Mbps, thus 1.3 Mbps is the maximum speed available.

3.4 Requirements of the automated office

Every system is designed for any number of reasons and, in order to be successful, or be at all useful, it must comply with at least one of these demands. The consideration of these requirements can be termed forming a model of the system. The more comprehensive the model, the better the eventual system will be.

The choice of the term 'model' has been carefully considered. Although an office automation system can be regarded as a distributed management information system, its analysis and design is difficult using the structured techniques discussed in later chapters. The main reason for this is the problems related to the electronic mail system. EMS concerns itself with *ad-hoc* messages which are difficult to define as regular data flows in terms of their content, their frequency and their destination. The structured techniques for analysis and design cannot easily cope with this irregularity and are therefore difficult to apply to an office automation system. Current research points towards the use of some form of computer-based model (possibly a simulation model) to specify the hardware and software requirements in terms of the network and the power of its nodes.

The original designers of the LANs had a number of ideas of the service that they should provide. However, as the use of LANs has developed, particularly with regard to office automation and EMSs, a number of previously unconsidered criteria have become evident. It should also be pointed out that the majority of LANs used for EMS were originally developed in, and for the use of, research establishments — a far cry from the commercial world.

3.4.1 Original requirements of LANs

The purpose behind the majority of research establishments' designs of LANs was to provide a system to link a number of remote devices in order that they might inter-communicate; the system was to provide:

- high data transmission rates
- low error rates
- easy physical connection of devices to the medium
- inexpensive transmission medium

These criteria have largely been satisfied in the LANs available today. However, while these factors are important to office automation and electronic mail, such systems demand a more complex model for full efficiency.

3.4.2 Recent developments

In two areas the manufacturers of LANs are making advances in an effort to provide an improved service.

Hybrid topologies

These systems have been developed primarily to spread the cost of a LAN interface over a number of terminals, and are expected to decline in popularity as the cost of LAN interfaces decreases. These hybrids consist basically of an Ethernet tree used to interconnect a number of multiplexors, to which terminals are attached in a star.

LAN–LAN interconnection

There is often a necessity, and advantages to be gained, in LAN–LAN interconnection. Organisations can have isolated LANs at remote office sites and yet be able to communicate between stations at these sites. The EMS becomes a much wider service. The development of 'gateways', specialised devices to convert the protocol of one network packet to the protocol of another, or a modification of internal communication structure of the interconnected system may well present solutions to the topology requirements to be presented in the following sections.

3.4.3 Requirements of electronic mail

The criteria concerning LANs are of extreme importance to EMS. However, even with these requirements catered for, a number of other factors can be considered in order that the ideal system, one that provides all the facilities required at a minimum cost and in the most efficient manner, can be provided. If it is accepted that present networks fulfil requirements with respect to transmission techniques, mediums and connective hardware, then the cost and efficiency factors can be directly related to topology and station-to-station communication.

Topology to match geography

Implementation of an EMS in an office block requires the selection of an available system, installation of the transmission medium and connection of the devices. In some situations the geographical distribution of the offices and hence the devices will lend itself to the physical and logical topology of the chosen LAN. That is, the offices with stations to be connected may exist as rooms off a long corridor; the ideal geography for an Ethernet. A single run of the bus down the corridor connecting to each station by means of drop cables. However, in the same situation, should a ring network be required, one half of the ring's medium may be redundant, doubling back on itself to complete the circuit. Of course, an environment where the stations are situated around the periphery of a regular-shaped building would be ideal for a ring system.

Unfortunately, situations where EMSs are to be installed are very often not geographically ideal. The most common situation will be one where the majority of stations can be reached without undue redundancy of cable but one or two stations, which need to be included, are remote from the others. The bus network, such as Ethernet, is rather more versatile than the ring, having the capability for spurring segments, joined by repeaters, also having drop cables from the bus to a device of up to 50 m. So the Ethernet could cope with the more awkward situations. However, the geographical layout of a site should not dictate the choice of system, since this is the prerogative of higher level demands.

The requirement of a model, in such situations, is that similar to the hybrid topologies mentioned in Section 3.4.2 where the benefits of a number of different topologies could be combined. A ring, for instance, having a node on the circuit which connected an Ethernet segment, or the branches of a star.

Using this technology, the LAN could be developed with optimum use of transmission media, but still retaining the full properties of the original systems from which the hybrid was derived.

Inter-station communication

All stations on a LAN are treated equally. No differentiation is made with regard to data flow from or to a particular node. In fact, care is taken in the design of the various systems to ensure that any one station cannot 'hog' the medium. Now it is quite likely that in an automated office communication between two, or a group of, nodes will normally exceed communication between the remainder of the nodes in total. It would seem reasonable that these high data flow channels should have some precedence over all others. As the transmission techniques have been set up, this is not possible or, within these systems, desirable — as any nodes with priority, and a large amount of data to transmit, would monopolise the system at the expense of all other nodes.

The requirement for this part of the model is for inter-station communications, within the network, but also as an isolated sub-network. That is, having identified a small number of stations which regularly communicate large amounts of data to each other, these stations should ideally be able to act as any other node on the network, that is to transmit and receive, from and to, all others on the system, but also to communicate with each other quite separately from the rest of the network. In this manner, devices that regularly converse with each other will not slow down transmission of all other devices on the system.

As EMSs develop, this area of LANs can be seen to be most important. Research is constantly proceeding for increases in bit rates, and with the links between high data flow devices eased, more efficient use will be made of the available rates by the network as a whole.

3.5 Summary

Although the technology of networking may not yet allow the type of modifications necessary to implement the requirements specified by the model, it would seem valid to indicate the manner in which the proposed factors should be considered. Having identified those requirements which need to be considered for an EMS model, clarification of how the model must use this information is necessary.

Of prime importance is identification of those stations requiring some form of extra-network communication. Having located these nodes, both their logical and physical position within the system must be considered. It is of little use identifying two stations in need of an extra link and then situating them at opposite ends of the network (although in some organisations this may well be unavoidable). Now the model can be seen to have a third requirement — the consideration of geographical placement of the stations. The positioning of offices is, of course, fixed by the constraints of the building, but the placing of particular stations in certain rooms allows some variation.

Thus it can be seen that the model must cater for three stages of implementation of the EMS. Primarily, defining the topology of the network to match the geographical layout of the stations to be served. In this way the system will be complete, that is all stations will have access to the transmission medium and the minimum amount of cabling will have been used. Secondly, stations needing extra inter-station communication must be identified. Data relating to the communication flow between stations must be collected, or hypothesised, allowances being made for the probable increase in data transmissions as users of the EMS become more familiar with the system. Finally, the positioning of stations within the environment must be arranged according to the findings of the second point. Where the EMS is to be implemented in a new situation, the positioning of nodes to meet the requirements of the model should pose few problems. However, the installation will often be in an established office environment, when the cost of straying from the ideal must be balanced against the disruption and trauma caused by moving personnel.

The technology needed to implement the proposed requirements is still very much under development. However, recognition of these needs will both indicate the direction research should take and also ensure that any suitable advances are swiftly implemented.

3.6 References

1. Gee, K. C. E. (1982). *Local Area Networks*, NCC.
2. Flint, D. C. (1983). *The Data Ring Main*, Wiley.

3. Thurber, K. J. and Freeman, H. A. (1979). 'Architecture considerations for local area computer networks', Proceedings of the International Conference on Distributed Computing Systems. Oct.
4. Metcalfe, R. M. and Boggs, D. R. (1976). 'Ethernet: distributed packet switching for local computer networks', Commun. ACM. Clark, D. D. *et al.* (1978). 'An introduction to local area networks', *Proc. IEEE*, Nov.
5. Gordon, B. (1980). 'Plying the Fast Post', *Computing*, May.

3.7 Bibliography

Cheong, V. E and Hirschheim, R. A. *Local Area Networks.*

Clark, D. D. (1978). 'An Introduction to LANs', *Proc. IEEE*, Nov.

Connel, S. and Galbraith, I. *The Electronic Mail Handbook.*

Edhart, J. L. (1981). *Understanding LANs*, Seybold, June.

Flint, O. C. *The Data Ring Main.*

Pritchard, J. A. and Wilson, P. A. *Planning Office Automation — Electronic Message System.*

Tanenbaum, A. S. (1981). *Computer Networks*, Prentice-Hall.

Welch, W. J. and Wilson, P. A. *Electronic Mail System — A Practical Evaluation Guide.*

CHAPTER 4

Developing an information system

4.1 Introduction

The design, development and implementation of a new management information system (MIS) is a major project to be undertaken by an organisation. The term project generally refers to a set of interrelated tasks leading towards some common objective and all projects can be treated as one-off. Clearly, the MIS project fits this description in that a number of stages are identifiable and these are summarised in Section 4.2.

The modern commercial environment is extremely competitive and in order to maximise profits and meet objectives all aspects of an organisation must be carefully managed. This is true in all spheres of business whether it is a factory, construction company or software house. When a company considers undertaking a project, a number of decisions must be made regarding the venture. One of the fundamental questions is to ascertain whether or not it will be profitable, and a significant variable here is the time-scale: 'time is money'. Thus, in order that a project does not run over time (and consequently budget) a high degree of control must be exercised. This control is part of a science termed project management. In the world of engineering, a number of techniques have been developed which assist in project management from the initial realisation of a scheme right through its subsequent life-cycle.

As computer projects become more numerous, both within the commercial environment, where computers are used as tools, and in the area of computer package development, it has become apparent that their control is an enigma to all levels of management. Projects are commenced without accurate estimates as to the cost, time-scale or resources necessary. Thus adequate control is virtually impossible.

4.2 Stages of development of information systems

Developing an information system (IS) is a complex project which itself requires careful management. As with all complex projects, the first thing to do is to break the work down into identifiable stages with deliverable items marking the end of each phase. All information system development projects can be broken down into the following stages:

● initiation
● justification
● analysis/investigation
● design
● development
● implementation
● post-implementation

There are two further activities which occur throughout the stages of the project and these are:

● testing
● documentation

4.2.1 Project initiation

The authorisation to start a project will come from the senior management of the organisation (the sponsors). It will take the form of an assignment brief to consider the feasibility of a new IS to overcome existing problems of:

● performance
● accuracy
● economy
● control
● efficiency
● security

which may exist with the existing system.

The assignment brief will instruct a project manager to set up a team to look at the justification for the project. The project manager will discuss and agree terms of reference with the sponsors which set out the 'deliverable items' for the initiation stage.

4.2.2 Justification

Project justification involves investigating the feasibility of a new IS in terms of technical and economic viability. It involves investigating:

- the realism of the terms of reference within the given constraints
- the functional operation of the organisation
- the IS requirements
- the need for improving the existing IS or designing a new one
- the costs and benefits of a proposed new system

It can be seen from this that, in a large organisation, the investigation of feasibility (commonly called the feasibility study) can involve a great deal of work. Typically, in British Telecom, a feasibility study into just one sub-system takes 2–3 man-years of effort. Smaller projects obviously involve less time but nevertheless a substantial commitment of resources is involved and the justification stage may be sub-divided into

(1) A *preliminary survey* which could well take several man-months and will assess whether a full feasibility study is worthwhile. If this is the case, the team will undertake:
(2) a full *feasibility study* which covers all the above areas and which is only completed with the production of a *feasibility study report*.

The feasibility study report will contain:

- terms of reference
- analysis of the functional system
- a summary of the requirement of the IS
- an outline description of a proposed IS
- estimates of costs, benefits and time-scales

The object of the report is to allow the project sponsors to decide whether or not to proceed with the proposal, to change the terms of reference, or abandon it.

4.2.3 Analysis and investigation

A certain amount of analysis of the existing IS and investigation of the requirements of any new system will have been done as part of the feasibility study. However, before the IS can be designed in detail, further work needs to be done in order to produce a detailed requirements report. This specifies:

- details of outputs required
- details of inputs available
- business procedures to be adopted
- computerised procedures necessary

- implementation and testing procedures
- detailed project budgets and plans

The requirements report is used as the basis for the design stage of the project.

4.2.4 System design

The design phase and subsequent phases will be discussed in detail in a later session. It involves using the requirements report to produce a detailed system specification which specifies, for the IS:

- all the input details (devices to be used, screen layouts, form design, contents and formats etc.)
- all the output details (devices to be used, screen layouts, form designs, report formats etc.)
- the files to be used (type, content, format, size etc.)
- the computer and associated manual procedures (description of algorithms, program structure, flow charts or logic diagrams etc.)

4.2.5 System development

Working with the detailed system specification, programmers construct the actual applications programs which control the IS. These are developed module by module and the resulting program code is thoroughly tested to ensure that it performs according to the detailed system specification. All the programs and procedures are fully documented along with test data and results.

4.2.6 Implementation

Once the system has been fully tested, it has to be introduced into the organisation. Files have to be converted, equipment installed, users trained, maintenance procedures developed etc. Most systems are phased in over a period of time with the old and the new systems running in parallel, and this requires careful planning and control.

4.2.7 Post-implementation

Once a system has been implemented, the work does not, unfortunately, stop. Organisations are dynamic and continue to evolve, and so must their information systems. Maintenance and enhancements are often required; systems are audited; environments change. All of these affect the life-cycle of the IS and must be accommodated until a total re-analysis and design is deemed necessary.

Stage	Deliverable item
Initiation	Terms of reference
Justification	Feasibility study report
Analysis/investigation	Requirements report
Design	Detailed system specification
Development	Working hardware and software
Implementation	Acceptance test results
Post-implementation	Maintenance/enhancement documentation

Figure 4.1

Although the typical stages listed above will be found within major projects undertaken by DP departments or consultancies, they may be given different names by individual organisations. The main point is that the stages and deliverable items are readily identifiable (see Figure 4.1).

4.3 Project management

Project management is intended to be a tool which will provide management with control over, and the flexibility to change, a project. Project management should give management:

- the ability to plan the best possible use of resources to meet a goal, given limits on time and cost
- the chance to plan 'one-off' projects, where experience cannot be gained from previous repetition or where standard time/cost information is unavailable
- information presented in a particularly easy-to-use fashion, such as time schedules, areas of slack time

As in all areas of management, there are many aspects to project management. However, here we restrict attention to those areas which relate directly to the quantitative aspects of the control of a project. Other areas of concern, such as staff management and equipment, are only considered when strictly relevant to a project as resources. Management must be involved with a project throughout its life-cycle, and as an aid to the necessary control each project may be divided into three specific areas of operation: feasibility, planning and control.

4.3.1 Feasibility

Initially every project comes to life as an idea, a vague plan to create a product or develop a situation. The original idea is subsequently massaged into shape until the final end product, and development scheme, is envisaged. Once the end product has been completely specified, in the form of agreed terms of reference, the control offered by project management may be applied to the project.

In order that decisions may be made regarding the viability of the product, all areas affected by the project must be considered. Intensive research must be undertaken in order that management may have accurate answers to questions concerning the proposed product, such as: is it profitable/ necessary/desirable in the interest of the company? In other words, does the project fit in with the strategic plans of the organisation? These answers, together with the estimated overall cost of the project, must be carefully considered. Only when sufficient research and investigation into the costs and benefits have provided management with a positive indication as to the feasibility of the project should its commencement be considered.

4.3.2 Planning

Subsequent to its approval, a project must be subjected to further control, as part of project management, before it is physically commenced. The complete life-cycle of the project must be considered, specified and planned. Ideally, the complete scheme will be defined as a number of interrelated, modular tasks, each of which must be assigned a time-scale, a cost, resource requirements and priority. Once the project has been defined in this manner, a reasonably accurate prediction may be made as to the total cost and time-scale of production (results from this planning may necessitate a return to the feasibility considerations, for further deliberation). This project plan will allow the definition of start and finish dates, the identification of tasks which must be completed before others are commenced and the scheduling of all necessary resources.

It is only by applying this type of control that a project may be commenced with confidence. Management will know exactly the manner in which a project is expected to proceed and may initiate the procedure with the knowledge that all areas of difficulty have been foreseen and allowances been made.

4.3.3 Control during the life-cycle

It is idealistic to assume that a well-planned project will adhere to a schedule throughout its life-cycle. It is an unfortunate fact of life that even the best of plans never run smoothly. Every project will have a large number of possible variables, any or all of which may change during its life-cycle. Equipment may malfunction, materials may not arrive on time, personnel may be taken ill—these few examples indicate the diversity of problems that may beset the management plan. However, some degree of control may be exercised over a 'rogue' project. If, for instance, a task is running over its allocated time-span, by dextrous manipulation of the original plan, devised as the ideal life-cycle of the project, new time-scales may be calculated for all tasks affected by the late running or, if possible, resources may be transferred to alleviate the problem. In either case the revised costs and completion dates can be readily calculated.

Use of the original plan, together with the latest information regarding the project, allows management to produce a new estimate of the project life-cycle when necessary, and thus ensure that continual optimal use is made of all resources — resulting in minimum costs. However, the fact that this degree of control is available does not negate the possibility that due to unfavourable circumstances a project may become infeasible, through the occurrence of extra costs or time-span. Being in an informed position and thus able to terminate a project during its life-cycle, if necessary, may be considered the ultimate level of control.

4.4 Long-range planning

Long-range or strategic planning is carried out as a matter of course in most organisations when considering their environment. The impetus behind strategic planning is an attempt to cope with:

(1) *Uncertainty* relating to unknown factors (for example, what will the economy be like in five years' time).
(2) *Complexity* relating to an understanding of how the environment operates.
(3) *Change* relating to the dynamics of the environment and the realisation that the situation in the future might be different to today's.

These factors influence the decision-making process and relate not only to organisational structures but also the information system's structure. The IS part of an organisation faces uncertainty, complexity and change through the dynamic interaction of three variables: the technology, the business needs and organisation needs, as shown in Figure 4.2.

At the technology end, it can be observed that hardware is becoming less expensive and at the same time more powerful. Also, new technologies such as expert systems, telecommunication, CAD/CAM and office systems are rapidly being introduced. Technology is, of course, used in organisations in order to satisfy business needs (that is, improving product quality and operational effectiveness) and organisational needs (that is, support within and between organisational units).

The effect of more powerful and cheaper hardware coupled to the capabilities of new technologies is that business and organisational needs demand an ever-increasing support by data-processing departments.

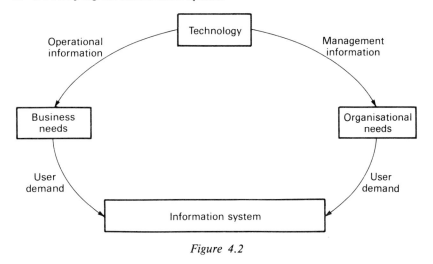

Figure 4.2

Therefore, planning for DP activities and adopting a methodical way for developing an IS is of crucial importance for the successful implementation of such a system.

4.5 Approaches to developing an IS

The developer of an IS is concerned with the identification and specification of functional and non-functional requirements and the transformation of the specification into computer models.

The development process is a series of model transformations, starting from those which are closer to the human perception and then gradually moving towards those which are close to the computer end. This view represents an idealistic situation but one which has been recognised as essential in order to devise systems which are effective and flexible.

Effectiveness implies that any system produced should satisfy the needs and objectives of the end-user. In particular, it should be sensitive to these needs and permit the user to view the system in a manner which is most natural to him. Flexibility implies that the system should be sensitive to changes in a user's viewpoint and should be easily adaptable, especially since the user's views and expectations will change over time.

The traditional approach to system development was a piecemeal approach in which applications were designed independently from each other. In contrast, today's systems are complex and therefore their development necessitates a different approach.

The underlying philosophy of traditional techniques is their concern with the identification and documentation of the flow of work through an organisation and the sequence of activities for achieving system objectives. No guide is given as to how these techniques may be used; instead an analyst uses his experience and know-how to derive a system specification. This specification is documented in the form of charts which, in turn, are supplemented by narrative.

Traditional techniques owe much to the way manual systems were observed and documented before the arrival of the computer. With the arrival of the computer and its application to business systems, analysts continued to use the same techniques usually with some minor modifications to suit the new type of usage. The increased scope and sophistication of today's systems necessitate methods for developing such systems, in radically different ways to those used for *ad-hoc* development.

The traditional approach to developing information systems is based on the idea that a problem exists and can be solved by the use of a computer. An application is considered in terms of its constituent functional parts. The result is the piecemeal computerisation of single applications. This method cannot be used successfully in complex areas such as the development of integrated systems.

There are a number of challenges that contribute to the necessity for a different approach to developing software systems. The main reasons are that:

(1) With the rapid price decrease witnessed over the past few years, hardware is no longer the focus of attention and therefore a developer should not be constrained to provide solutions which are guided by hardware considerations.
(2) There is an acute shortage of skilled personnel resulting in ever-increasing pressure on data-processing departments which inevitably fail to keep up with user demand for the provision of computer-based solutions.
(3) There is a host of new types of application emerging such as decision support systems, expert systems, office systems etc.
(4) The late delivery, excessive cost, inflexibility and unreliability of delivered systems result in user dissatisfaction and often rejection of these systems.

These challenges, coupled to the problems associated with the complexity of present-day information systems have highlighted the inadequacy of the informal way of building such systems. The response has been the emergence of a number of software development methods which recognise the need for a well-structured development process.

4.6 System development methods

An information system development method is an attempt to formalise the development process. A method will have:

- an underlying philosophy about the representation of a system (conceptual model)
- a set of techniques
- a set of tools which are to be used in conjunction with the techniques for the derivation of a conceptual model
- procedures on how to use the tools
- procedures on planning and controlling the development process
- allocation of people to tasks
- documentation about the method.

The objective of a software development method is two-fold. First, it attempts to provide the management structures necessary for the planning and control of the development process. And secondly, it attempts to improve the quality of the software produced by providing a formalism for the specification of the system.

Many software development methods currently exist.[1,2] These methods encourage the use of semi-formal rules, generally follow a top-down approach and use graphical notation to enhance the 'visibility' of a system specification.

Most of the methods (certainly those most popular in industry) follow one of two philosophies: process-oriented or data-oriented. However, despite their proclaimed differences, there has been over the past few years a great shift from both camps towards finding a common ground and there is no longer a clear distinction between the two approaches. Processes and data need to be considered with equal importance when developing a software system and therefore such a common view seems to be attractive both in theory and in practice. The issues discussed in this book are considered with this common view in mind.

4.7 Summary

The rate of change in computer technology and the complexity of contemporary business systems means that the development of an IS which uses such a technology to support the organisation requires careful planning and control. It has been argued in this chapter that planning and control should be applied during the development of a project in:

(1) managing organisational resources (people, technology etc.) by following a set of techniques for planning and reviewing the progress of the development; and

(2) improving the effectiveness and flexibility of the delivered system by following a methodical way in understanding and documenting the nature of the required IS.

Issues relating to (1) are covered in Chapter 5 whereas those of (2) are discussed in Chapters 6 and 7.

4.8 References

1. CRIS (1982). 'Information Systems Design Methodologies: A Comparative Preview', *Proc. IFIP TC8 Working Conference on Comparative Review of Information Systems Design Methodologies*, Noodijkerhout, The Netherlands, 10–14 May, North Holland.
2. Maddison, R. N. *et al.* (1983). *Information System Methodologies*, Wiley Heyden Ltd.

CHAPTER 5

Information system project management

5.1 Introduction

Experience has shown that successful information system (IS) development can only be achieved by applying appropriate techniques which assist in the management of the project.

There are a number of well-established techniques available which assist in project management. These techniques have been developed primarily in the engineering field and thus relate particularly well to that environment. It will be seen that some of these techniques relate specifically to the areas of project management outlined previously and others are concerned with the same areas, but differ widely in the number of project variables that they address. No attempt has been made in this chapter to give a full description of any of the techniques listed below; any further information may be obtained from other texts.[1,2,3,4]

This chapter deals with the techniques which are used for:

- formulating estimations of time requirements
- monitoring progress
- comparing actual against planned performance

5.2 Project management techniques

These techniques can be categorised under the following:

- overall resource management
- management of programming and physical development of the system
- review of progress

5.2.1 Decision criteria

The theories of decision are used solely during the feasibility study of a project. Their use requires estimations of the anticipated profitability of, or benefit to be gained from, the end product of a project, and the cost of the project overall.

Decision criteria encompass a number of differing techniques, for example, decision theory, maximin criteria, regret criteria.[4] Each allows the user to place emphasis upon his own expectations of the market situation and thus decisions are made having taken note of the real possibilities of fluctuating markets. By using decision criteria, together with management experience, optimal courses of action may be calculated from the estimated figures provided. Hence conclusions as to the real viability of a project may be reached. It should be noted that other project management techniques[5] may need to be applied to a project before any decision criteria are used, due to the requirement of an accurate estimation of total project cost, for use as input to the decision theories in use.

5.2.2 Milestone charts (project status report)

The use of milestone charts involves the division of a project into separate, self-contained tasks. A table, or chart, is then drawn up listing these tasks plus relevant information concerning each one. Each tuple of the table will contain such items as the task title, employee or team assigned, a review date and the completion date. Figure 5.1 illustrates a typical milestone chart.

The milestone charts provide a convenient, easily prepared and understood reference table. A quick glance at the table will provide management with basic information about each modular task. However, while use of the chart will indicate whether a job has overrun its expected completion date, there is no way that this can be used to assess the overall effect that this will have on the project as a whole.

In fact, milestone charts do not indicate the interrelationships between tasks, that is overlap of tasks or tasks which must be completed before another can be commenced. A further limitation of milestone charts can be seen as their lack of provision for any other variables than time; resource scheduling or costs are not catered for.

Project Status Report

System Title ....

Page .... of ....

Date issued ....

Task No.	Task Desc.	Staff Responsible	Original Estimate			Latest Estimate			Next Review
			Man-Days	Start	Completion	Man-Days	Start	Completion	
. . . 5	Produce Manuscript	Clare, Loucopoulos	200	1/2/85	30/11/85	300	1/3/85	31/5/86	3/4/86
6	Edit Manuscript	A. N. Other	10	6/12/85	20/12/85	10	7/6/86	20/6/86	3/9/86
. . .	. . .	. . .	. . .	. . .	. . .	. . .	. . .	. . .	. . .

Signed ....

Figure 5.1

5.2.3 Gantt charts

Gantt charts, named after their originator, are very similar to milestone charts. Tasks are defined in the same manner and tabulated on the chart. The time-span of each task is indicated by the length of a line drawn on an adjacent calendar. The calendar is defined in the scale chosen to be the most appropriate by the project manager, hours, days, weeks etc. Figure 5.2 illustrates such a chart.

The advantages, and disadvantages, of Gantt charts are similar to those specified for milestone charts. They are easy to prepare and understand and although they can illustrate the overlap of tasks by the definition of start and finish times on the calendar, predecessor tasks are still not identified, nor can the effect of delays be related to the project as a whole.

5.2.4 Networks

Networking is a generic name for a number of techniques which utilise what is termed 'time network analysis' as a basis for the control of manpower, resources and capital used in a project. The indiscriminate switching of one technique name for another in many publications has resulted in much confusion as to which name refers to which technique. Before a description of the networking technique is attempted, a brief recount of its history may help alleviate this problem.

In 1958 the Special Projects Office of the US Navy, concerned with performance in large development projects, introduced a Project Evaluation and Review Technique (PERT) on its Polaris weapon system. At about the same time the US Airforce developed a similar system called Project Evaluation Procedure (PEP), although this was subsequently dropped in favour of PERT. Dupont, the large chemical concern, in an effort to shorten the length of time between product research and production, initiated a study which resulted in a technique known as critical path method, or analysis (CPM/CPA).

At the time of their conception, both PERT and CPA were virtually the same system. Both these project management techniques were concerned solely with the time-span of a project's tasks, their interrelation and, hence, the life-cycle of the project as a whole.[6]

As the engineering community became aware of the obvious benefits of PERT/CPA they were further developed in order that the control offered by these techniques could encompass more of the variables that exist as part of a large project. It is at this point that the beginning of the differentiation between PERT and CPA can be identified. While CPA was to remain unchanged, that is dealing with time factors only, PERT was developed by various academic and commercial bodies to encompass an increasing

Planning and Progressing Chart

Page .... of ....

Date issued ....

System Title ....

Task No.	Task Desc.	Slippage	Time Periods (months)																				
			J	F	M	A	M	J	J	A	S	O	N	D	J	F	M	A	M	J	J	A	S	O
							1985									1986								
5	Produce manuscript	−1m																						
6	Edit manuscript	−6m																						
7	Arrange type-setting contract																							
8	Arrange printing contract	. . . .																						
. . . .	. . . .																							

▨ Actual

◼ Estimate

Signed ....

Figure 5.2

number of other project variables. The decision regarding which of the two techniques to work on was, apparently, quite arbitrary.

The development of PERT has been described as a number of successive generations:

(1) *First generation:* PERT/TIME, the original specification, virtually identical to CPA.
(2) *Second generation:* PERT/COST, the effects and consequences of any divergence from the planned time-scale are related to overall costings.
(3) *Third generation:* PERT/LOB (line of balance), where the utilisation of a time-orientated network is used for planning the project, but more specifically as a management information system (MIS) during the production phase of the project.
(4) *Fourth generation:* PERT/LOB/COST, used to take into account time, cost and resource scheduling. One published fourth-generation PERT is known as CSPC (cost and schedule planning and control)[8] and is claimed not only to serve as a control mechanism for project managers but is also designed to enhance executives' visibility of the project.

While definitions of the later generations of PERT are not always as rigorous as one would hope, the general concept being developed in order to accommodate an increasing number of project factors under its umbrella of control is fairly clear.

Having highlighted these variations in network techniques, it should be noted that however high one climbs on the PERT generation ladder, the basic networking procedure remains the same; in particular, all define a critical path. As the complexity of the technique increases, more parameters are simply included in the basic scheme. For this reason it is deemed prudent to include all the networking systems, that is CPA and all the PERT generations, under the banner of PERT (an arbitrary choice). This will dispel confusion. When the term PERT is used in the remainder of this chapter, the degree of complexity of the technique will either be apparent from the text, or will be a generalisation to cover any variations deemed appropriate.

As indicated above, the basic PERT technique relates solely to time-scales. In order to apply PERT to a project, the complete scheme must initially be split into a number of self-contained tasks. Predictions as to the time-span of each task must then be made. Tasks which must be finished before others may commence must be identified and either a start date or target date for the finish of the complete project must be set (one is set, the other obviously being governed by the total life-cycle of the project, calculated with the aid of the completed network).

The heart of any PERT analysis is the network, or arrow diagram (see Figure 5.3). This differs significantly from the Gantt charts. The diagram

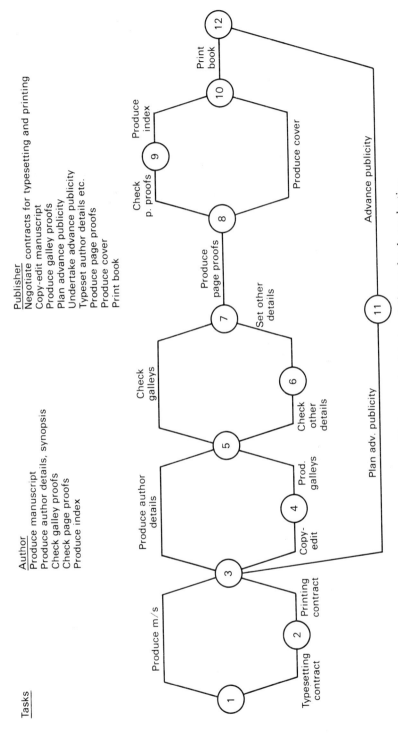

Tasks

Author
Produce manuscript
Produce author details, synopsis
Check galley proofs
Check page proofs
Produce index

Publisher
Negotiate contracts for typesetting and printing
Copy-edit manuscript
Produce galley proofs
Plan advance publicity
Undertake advance publicity
Typeset author details etc.
Produce page proofs
Produce cover
Print book

Figure 5.3 Simplified network of tasks relating to book production

consists of a number of circles (events) which indicate the start or completion of a task, and arrows (activities) representing the tasks themselves.

Having introduced the network diagram, and before any further description, a concept is introduced here which is developed in a later section: the comparison of structured analysis and design (Chapter 6).

The network can be said to follow similar principles to the data flow diagram (DFD) occurring in structured systems analysis and design methodologies.[9] Each event is displayed as a circle with vectors 'input' to and 'output' from that event. The diagram shows, at each point, the status of a project in that an event relies upon a certain number of activities (inputs) which themselves rely on previous events. Furthermore, subsequent activities (shown as outputs from a particular event) cannot commence until that event has occurred. DFDs involve the use of circles to represent processes which require and produce input and output data flows. A process cannot start until all its inputs are present and no outputs can occur until the process is activated.

The parallel between the network and the DFD is rather more than just appearance. Both are static diagrammatic representations of a dynamic system, representing that system as a series of sub-systems each with well-defined inputs and outputs. Because of the structure of the diagrams, effects of modification of inputs and outputs to a particular node (circle) can be related to the entire structure which, in PERT terms, means the entire project span. Both techniques also suffer from the fact that the more complex the project, the more difficult is the construction of the diagram. With DFDs this problem is overcome by the technique of 'levelling' the diagram. The first stage is to create a context-level diagram showing one large process with a mass of data input flows and a mass of outputs. The context diagram is then sub-divided into levels of refinement where each circle is successively replaced by a number of linked circles reflecting the refinement of one process into a number of sub-processes. This technique is well documented by De Marco[9] and further elaborated in Chapter 6.

It is probable that this levelling technique could be adapted for the construction of a PERT network diagram. The main difference would be that the successive refinement process would be concentrated more on the lines (activities) than the circles (events). Levelling DFDs, although concentrating on the circles (processes), necessarily carries along the subdivision of the lines (data flows) as an integral part of the exercise. PERT diagram 'levelling' would be in a sense the reverse of this but, if successful, would result in a properly structured system of activities and events. The levelling methodology for PERT is an area for further research.

Having brought the apparent similarities between structured analysis and design and PERT techniques to the fore, a more complete description of the network analysis follows.

Two events are linked by means of an activity, the arrows are not drawn to any scale, but the time-span of the activity is included, as a figure, above the arrow. By careful construction of the diagram, the interdependence of one task upon another is illustrated; that is, for a task (activity) to be shown as being the predecessor of another, an arrow is drawn linking the circle which indicates the start of the predecessor to the circle indicating the start of its dependant. 'Dummy' activities are used to distinguish between the activities associated with an event which has more than one dependant; these 'dummy activities' are normally of zero duration.

Having constructed the diagram and indicated activity time-spans, the network is subjected to forward analysis, when each event is given an earliest start time (earliest event time (EET)) based on the duration of the activities preceding it. The critical path (CP) may now be identified: this is the longest direct route through the network, that is, lengthening the time-span of any of the activities on the CP would extend the EET of the final event. The network can now be reverse analysed, calculating the latest event time (LET) for each event, that is, the latest time an event may occur without affecting the EET of the final event (this would in fact alter the route of the CP). The network can now be said to be 'time-analysed'. Figure 5.4 illustrates this process. For the details of the calculations, the reader should refer to the references.

Reference to this time-analysed network supplies immediate information as to the effect of a task overrun. Those tasks on the CP will, obviously, have a direct effect upon the complete project time-span. Such tasks are practically identified as those whose EET and LET coincide. However, all other tasks will have a 'float', or 'slack quantity', which is the amount of time that their LET differs from their EET; that is, any overrun which is less than or equal to their slack quantity will not alter the project life-span.

Any alteration to a task's estimated time-span can conveniently be checked against the network which can easily be recalculated to compensate for any unexpected occurrences. The effect of resource rescheduling is also readily modelled, 'what if?' type enquiries may be posed and readily answered by appropriately restructuring the network.

Although this description has dealt solely with the consideration of time-spans, it is evident that factors such as cost and resource scheduling can be incorporated into this technique, forming an extremely powerful, albeit complex, project management tool.

5.3 Evaluation of techniques

Most of the advantages and disadvantages of the various techniques were considered in the section concerned with their descriptions. Hence this evaluation exists primarily as a summary of the major functions concerning

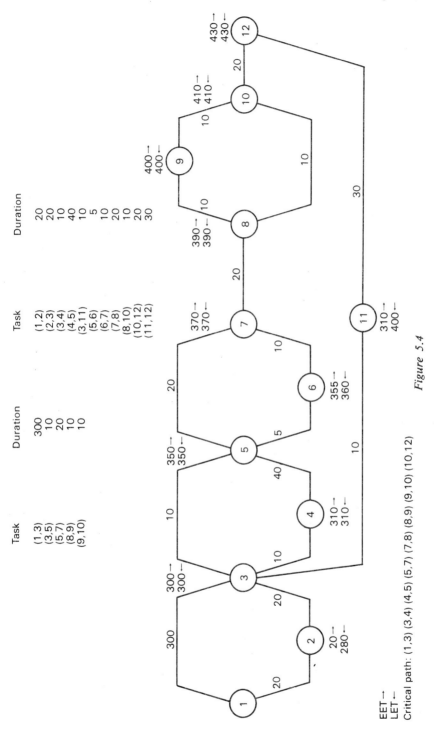

Figure 5.4

the use and versatility of these techniques as aids to successful project management.

Decision criteria are a number of well-specified, established theories. However complex the theory itself, the necessary input is relatively simple (which does not imply that arriving at that input data is not a complex procedure based upon a combination of information, intuition and experience). The theories of decision require, as input, a calculation or estimation of the cost of the project and the benefit to be gained from the end product of that project. Given these parameters, it is obvious that any product, regardless of discipline (engineering, construction, computing etc.), may be successfully appraised using decision criteria.

Milestone and Gantt charts may be considered as useful in the planning stages of a project but, due to their general restrictions in demonstrating the many facets of task interrelationships, are found to be limited in their use as a project control medium. Compared with the more complex network analysis diagrams, milestone and Gantt charts are easily prepared but as a source of information and subsequent control they may be deemed outmoded.

Successful network analysis provides management with a source of varied, reliable information; interrelationships of tasks are readily seen, time-scales and the effect of overruns are easily calculated, complete networks are simply adapted should unexpected variations occur, or simply to answer 'what-if?' queries. From the use of basic CPA through successive generations of PERT, project control is offered to management, the choice of techniques being governed by the degree of variables to be monitored.

5.4 Software tools for project management

In November 1982, *Engineering Computers*[10] declared that computer manufacturers had 'at last' realised the potential in the engineering field and published a synopsis of available management packages, several of these being specifically for project management.

The range of software would appear to be comprehensive, starting with cheap packages for micros and extending to systems with prices in the five-figure bracket. Some industries have developed software specific to their own field while others have the advantage of packages from software houses catering for a particular industrial field, or a particular aspect of project management. The CEGB's Smart 2, which tackles the project management of repairs, maintenance and construction at power stations, is claimed to produce optimum, rather than the fastest, scheduling, the emphasis being on work continuity. Systems exist which may be used in project planning, financial modelling and resource procurement. For example, the PPC system allows the tracking of a project's progress against the original plan, making adjustments and analysing the effects that they have. Other systems have been designed specifically for oil companies, architects and construction companies. Although these systems are specific to their respective users, the majority of packages available are intended for use in a wide range of situations and thus address the problems of project management in a more general fashion.

While an intensive study has not been carried out it would appear that, in common with most commercial purchases, the more expensive products provide a more complete and complex service. So while the cheaper micro-based packages may provide only the basic PERT (time analysis) and place restrictions on the number of events and activities specified, the more costly software designed for larger machines will offer increasing levels of processing features, for example, cost, resources, dates, holiday factors etc. Similarly, graphical output will improve from basic network drawing to include graphs, bar charts and histograms.

It should be noted that there is, apparently, no software available to support decision criteria, although a number of algorithms have been published[11] for completing this task, the majority being iterative tasks ideally suited for interaction between the decision maker, the analyst and a computer.

Although the computer software industry has only recently become aware of the market for project management packages, the range of products now available allow management the opportunity to make full use of the established PERT technique. The speed and ease with which computer-based networks may be set up, adjusted and re-analysed allows general 'what if?' queries and run-time control to become a true real-time possibility.

5.5 Tailoring an engineering project to PERT

As indicated previously, all references to network analysis techniques shall be couched under the general heading of PERT. The number of parameters used in specifying a project will be the means of identifying the level of PERT to be used.

In order that a project be controlled in the most effective manner, it must be analysed and tailored to suit the management technique. Initially, once defined, a project must be divided into a number of tasks. Each task should ideally be small enough to allow the reliable estimation of time, cost etc.

but large enough to be seen as a complete activity with well-defined start and finish points. This part of the project analysis is perhaps the most critical, as the omission of any activity will nullify any accuracy of the final plan and addition of a task at a later date would necessitate the complete reworking of the network. Thus care must be taken to include all tasks which are ancillary to those more easily recognised. These might include:

- preparation of materials
- ordering and delivery of materials
- testing of completed parts
- training of end-product users
- writing of manuals
- clearing away of waste materials

Having identified all tasks which make up the total project, each must be allocated a time-scale. Many jobs within the engineering and construction industries are well practised and hence estimates as to their time-span may be performed accurately, based on experience. However, when previous knowledge is non-existent or unreliable, algorithms exist which enable the calculation of reasonably accurate estimations.

In order to complete the basic network, tasks which are predecessors of others must be identified. Once these processes have been completed, the network may be drawn up and time analysis performed on the project as a whole. Thus prepared, the network will allow identification of the CP (the path linking all those tasks whose time-scales control the overall project time-scale) and the slack areas (the tasks which may overrun their estimated time-scale without delaying the end point of the project).

This is the most basic PERT technique; planning and control are catered for but purely with respect to time. Further parameters may be added to each task, in order that costs and various resources may be accounted for. Cost may be related to a number of aspects of a task including manpower, materials, use of machinery and use of space. Consideration must also be given to inflation if the project life-cycle extends over one year. By careful manipulation of resources, extra costs, due to a project running behind schedule, may be minimised. This is the concept termed resource scheduling where resources (labour, capital, materials, working area etc.) are moved from one task to another. For instance, a task which is overrunning may be allocated resources from one which has a large slack period. The network will assist in ensuring that any manipulations result in as little cost effect as possible.

It can be seen that an engineering project with tasks conveniently specified and time-scales accurately estimatable, due to long-term repetition and experience, is ideally suited to the PERT techniques of project planning and control.

5.6 Tailoring a computer project to PERT

Computer projects have been in existence for a relatively short time compared to other forms of engineering project and consequently management have little intuitive reasoning or expertise to apply to them. Whereas long-term repetition, and subsequent experience, in construction and similar industries allow the reasonably accurate estimation of project variables such as time, cost and resources required, faced with an equivalent computer project, management apparently have little idea of time-scales or cost. Thus project control is to all intents and purposes practically non-existent, leading to inadequate communication between those involved, over-extended time-scales and costs and the eventual high probability of inadequate end-product delivery.

It is obvious that some form of project management is required for application to computer projects and, as PERT is successfully used by engineering management, investigations should be made into its suitability for computer projects. Having previously identified the processing necessary to fit an engineering project to PERT, a computer project will need to undergo the same analysis.

5.6.1 Division into tasks

The primary concern must be to split the whole project into tasks, using the same criteria to judge the size of each as for an engineering project, that is, small enough to allow accurate time-scale estimation but large enough to be identified as a complete and definable job.

The advent and promotion of structured analysis and programming may well be viewed as an aid to defining a project in the required manner. The benefits of the various methods of structured analysis and design[9,12,13,14] have mainly been expressed with a view to the quality of the end product. By taking the overall 'problem' of the need for a new information system and proceeding through the process of successive refinement, the analyst eventually ends up with a series of sub-problems all with clearly-defined interfaces. This 'divide and conquer' approach allows the sub-problems to be tackled systematically in the knowledge that as each is solved, providing the interface definitions have been maintained, then the aggregation of the solutions should lead to a correct comprehensive solution to the initial problem.

The structured approach can (and should) be applied at all stages throughout the analysis, design and development of an information system. The end product of this approach is usually more reliable in its operation and, more importantly, it is more flexible as regards the ease of maintenance and enhancement. Thus the structured methodologies result in considerable cost savings over the lifetime of an information system.

These benefits provide a strong enough argument for the use of structured methodologies, but the project manager can further exploit the PERT approach. The process of successive refinement naturally produces self-contained modules of work whether at the analysis, design or development stages. Such modules fit the requirements of the first stage of PERT in that their content (tasks) is established as well as the control aspects such as preparation and reviews being specified. As in engineering projects, care must be taken in order that no tasks are overlooked. Processes such as making appointments for interviews, preparations for presentations and walkthroughs (at specific stages in the life-cycle of the project) must not be overlooked, and carefully included in the list of tasks.

While it may be seen as a painstaking and tedious process, the sectioning of a computer project into separately defined tasks may be seen as relatively problem free, given the tools available and a stoical approach to the problem.

5.6.2 Estimation of time-scales

The next stage in the PERT process is to estimate task time-scales and, while the specifying of the tasks themselves may be expected to present few problems, the accurate estimations of their times will be seen to be widespread with difficulties. De Marco[9] notes the difficulties inherent in these estimations, pointing out that data regarding past projects is rarely collected, and admitting that estimating within structured analysis is heuristic. This is far from the accuracy required for a successful PERT.

Many formal approaches at estimating time-scales for computer system projects have been tried over the past twenty years. Very few have met with any success, although the 'best' methods are described below. However, most practitioners tend to favour 'guesstimating' rather than estimating. This usually involves combining a hunch for the 'feel' of the particular project with some form of comparison with similar jobs undertaken in the past.

This approach was often acceptable in the second and third generation of computer information systems. Then, most projects were concerned with the computerisation of a specific task or of the work of a specific department within an organisation. For example, a project would be to develop a computerised payroll system. If the project manager had had previous experience of computerising payrolls, then the previous development times (possibly adjusted for the size of the organisation) were regarded as good an estimate as any. This somewhat sloppy approach is very dangerous with fourth-generation information systems (see Chapter 8) where the entire corporate information system is the scope of the project. Under these circumstances, payroll is but a part of a complete information system which will have many aspects peculiar to the organisation in question. Clearly the 'wet-finger-in-the-air' approach is not acceptable.

As an aid in estimating the time-scale of an activity, the engineering users of PERT developed a method for providing an 'accurate estimate'.[3] Initially, three estimates are made:

- *To:* an optimistic time-scale
- *Tm:* the most likely time-scale
- *Tp:* a pessimistic time-scale

Now in order to arrive at the time-scale to be used (*Te*):

$$Te = (To + 4Tm + Tp)/6$$

However, a number of authorities question the accuracy of this estimate and point out that the majority of estimates tend to be optimistic. Thus a normal distribution curve will not predict the spread of estimating errors. The following alternative is suggested:

$$Te = (To + 3Tm + 2Tp)/6$$

While the above method may well provide a reasonably accurate estimation of time-scales for a number of activity types, there are in fact a number of more fundamental problems within a computer project which can be identified.

5.6.3 Data collection

A large part of analysis consists of data collection, which is often effected by interviewing the personnel with direct knowledge of the information required. Before considering the number of estimates necessary to calculate an 'accurate estimate', consideration should be given to the question: Can an estimate be made regarding the length of time needed to obtain information, in an interview? A number of factors can be seen to affect these situations. The amount of data to be collected will have a bearing upon the length of the interview, but more relevant may be the interaction between the interviewer and interviewee. The situation where an interviewer is able to specify his requirements and the interviewee understands exactly what is required from him, will result in a shorter interview than the equivalent situation when the interviewee is at a loss as to what is required from him and the interviewer is unable to convey his needs.

A further difficulty with estimating the time required for fact-finding concerns the attitudes and reactions of the user staff to be interviewed. Much depends on the formal and informal industrial relations atmosphere within the organisation and this, in turn, depends on the management style in operation. People are naturally resistant to any change unless they are convinced that they, personally, will benefit from that change. The whole idea of 'computerisation' represents a major change and, moreover, it has to be said that this has a poor record in terms of publicity.

Many people tend to regard computers as a threat. Middle-management grades tend to worry about their career prospects: the computer takes away their decision-making responsibilities; all the expertise that they have built up over the years will go to waste; they will at best become button-pushers and at worst join the ranks of unemployed professionals. Administrative and clerical staff regard computers as direct replacements taking away their jobs and prospects. Secretaries see their jobs being degraded to printer-minders and so on. Much of this is, in fact, myth and it is the job of management to dispel such myths and to convince staff of the positive benefits of computerisation, including the fact that it often enhances job prospects.

If this 'selling' job is not done, however, the staff will resist the change, and this can manifest itself during information-gathering exercises. Staff will consciously or subconsciously withhold information, mislead the interviewer or make the interview difficult. Very often this will result in interviews taking much longer than previously estimated, or even repeat interviews.

Given these unpredictable complexities in interactions between people and the manner in which some information requirements are hidden beneath layers of surplus data, it is unlikely that even use of the method previously mentioned would succeed in providing an accurate time-scale for interviews.

5.6.4 Coding

In complete contrast to the problems encountered in data collection, the process of coding a program or program module may be completely structured. However, difficulties in estimating time-scales still abound. Again use may be made of the aforementioned time-scale estimating method (there are methods directly relating to coding that are described later). However, coding of a program is a skilled task and therefore programmers of varying experience and expertise will work at differing rates. In estimating the time for a section of code, the project manager/leader may make an unrealistic estimate if the task is to be processed by an inexperienced programmer. Should the manpower for a complete project be allocated their tasks at an early stage in order that they might give their own time-estimates? In this case, would a junior programmer have the experience necessary to make a realistic estimate?

With the development of software for a computerised information system, the problems of producing a good product are well researched and documented. The whole area of software engineering aims to provide methodologies designed to ensure that a software product is proven prior to its completion and hence the rigorous testing should confirm that the software meets its specification. Thus the aim is to produce software of good quality and this is an area of debate. The quality of software is difficult to measure; attempts have been made to define quality at a number of levels but there are a wide range of views within the software engineering fraternity as to what such measures should be.

With second- and third-generation computing, the standard measure used in estimating time requirements was the number of lines of code. Hence a piece of software could be estimated as 5000 lines (of monolithic code), the programmer productivity rate was 10 lines of working tested code per day and hence 500 days were required. With a number of programmers working on the code, without having clearly-defined modules to code, and without working to engineering standards, it is not difficult to see why such estimates were unreliable. In addition to this there was no attempt to assess the quality of code; a good programmer could probably write 100 lines of 'bad' code in a day and may be tempted to do so as the deadline approaches.

The research on software engineering aims at easing this problem by defining the ways in which quality code can be produced. Until such standards are widely adopted, the estimating of time (and hence resources) will still be difficult.

As previously indicated, there are formulae which profess to give an estimate for coding time, and two are presented here. The first from S. Wooldridge:[2]

(1) Count the number of files to be handled by the program.
(2) Count the number of records to be processed.
(3) Count the number of processing modules or pages of coding required.
(4) Let $S = 1 + 2 + 3$.
(5) Determine the complexity, C, as follows:
$S < 70$ then $C = 2.5$ (ave/easy)
$70 < S < 200$ then $C = 4$ (ave/difficult)
$S > 200$ then $C = 5.5$ (difficult/impossible)
(6) Calculate: $(S*23)/60 + (C*S)/24$

This result gives programming time in man-days, assuming a programmer of average ability and a working day of 6 hours.

The second method is the basic COCOMO model from B. W. Boehm:

$$MM = 2.4(KDSI)^{\wedge}1.05$$

where MM = man-months (19 man-days)
$KDSI$ = thousand delivered source insts.

The COCOMO model, in fact, goes on to extremely complex classifications of software for use in adapting the basic model.

It is interesting to note that before any of these formulae can be used, a number of estimates have to be made such as files to be handled, records accessed or lines of code. Any inaccuracies in these figures will of course affect the final result — erroneous estimates compounding to form an inaccurate estimate. These methods of estimating time-scales are regarded with suspicion and generally considered as purely academic. In fact, it can be regarded as a 'chicken and egg' paradox; if one knows the number of lines of code, then one can calculate the time required but one does not know the size of the product until it is completed.

Having cast doubts upon the accuracy of the above time-estimating methods, it is of interest to record the findings of a colleague with regard to the COCOMO model.

A 1500 line program was written, taking 70 days to produce. Applying the COCOMO model to this program, and assuming that KDSI is the equivalent to 1000 lines of code, the estimated time to code the program would be 3.67 man-months or 69.73 man-days. It would appear that in this case the model compared well with reality but whether this is an exception or the norm is unknown. Further research into these time-scale models is necessary before any definite recommendations may be made.

5.6.5 Resource scheduling

The primary resource for a computer project is manpower. Other facilities, including hardware availability, may have relevance in many instances, but this section limits its considerations to the scheduling of manpower.

Resource scheduling is employed in project management in two ways, initially when decisions are made as to teams that will work on various tasks and, secondly, when control of a project, during its life-cycle, makes rescheduling necessary. Allocating manpower at the planning stage of the project is of particular importance, because in this manner the abilities of personnel may be put to their most profitable use. Perhaps of equal importance is the movement of resources (manpower) from one task to another when to do so will hasten the completion of a task behind schedule, or in some way improve the running of the project as a whole.

In some forms of 'hard' engineering projects it is possible to increase resources on a particular task with a view to shortening the elapsed time for that task. Put simplistically, if a task time-scale is set at 20 man-days, then 1 man will take 20 days, 2 men 10 days and so on. This can be achieved for certain types of work, as in construction, but it is by no means universal. Moreover, there are many projects (including all software development projects) where adding twice as many people does not halve the time. The man-month as a unit of 'currency' is in fact a myth.[15] In software projects the structure of the system determines the number of modules and it is often useful to assign the development of one module to one programmer. The addition of extra programmers tends to increase the communications and hence the management problems. Taken to extremes, there comes a point when the addition of extra staff in fact lengthens the project.

5.6.6 Costing

Given a task, the length of time to complete it and the resources necessary, the costing of that task is a straightforward process. However, as has been indicated, arriving at the relevant, accurate estimates is far from easy. Unfortunately the accuracy of the project costings is heavily reliant upon these estimates and thus becomes yet another problem area.

5.6.7 Looping processes

Within structured analysis, or any other efficient analysis method, there exists a number of situations where loops within a process can occur. Principal areas where process looping is often necessary are:

- presentation of system specification to the user
- during program testing
- presentation of the completed system

At each of these stages during a computer project life-cycle the analysis should allow for the possible occurrence of unforeseen problems or modifications required. These situations will all require a return to an earlier stage in the project life-cycle, modifications made and a subsequent retracing of the original path through the project. For instance, when presented with the system specification the user may realise the need for processing that was originally unspecified. This change to the system requirements may necessitate further data collection, hence interviewing. Having completed the necessary work and incorporated it into the overall scheme, the analyst returns once more to the user for approval of the system design. This process may not occur as an isolated instance, but only when the end user is satisfied may the cycle of the project continue. Similarly, during program testing bugs may be found, requiring the recording of some modules. Only when all tests are successful may the cycle continue.

Unfortunately, PERT does not cater for loops. The conditional looping, which is an important part of structured analysis, cannot be incorporated into a network diagram, nor into the network analysis.

Thus having specified the tasks, estimated time-scales and costs and allocated resources, PERT may be used to perform network analysis upon the project, and thus provide planning and control. However, as soon as a situation which requires backtracking through the project (looping) occurs, the system of control breaks down. In such situations the PERT network may still be used by modifying the subsequent time-scales in order to take account of the delay. However, this is of little use when the original estimates of the critical path, slack periods and project end time are made.

5.7 Personnel management

This section discusses the issues relating to the management of personnel throughout the development process. In particular, three different approaches to organising development teams will be discussed: chief programmer teams; specialist teams; and leaderless teams.

5.7.1 Chief programmer teams

The chief programmer team consists of a chief programmer, a backup programmer and support personnel. Such a structure is shown in Figure 5.5.

The chief programmer is a highly qualified and experienced programmer who is assigned the following tasks:

- design program and test all critical systems modules
- integrate and test the team's programs
- act as the primary contact between users and development teams

The main drive behind the chief programmer team approach is to enable staff at senior level to remain at the mainstream programming effort rather than being moved up to a (usually) non-technical managerial level. This approach provides the opportunity for a technical person to continue in a development role.

A backup programmer has similar skills to the chief programmer but usually less experience. Such a person performs the tasks of:

- researching design alternatives
- researching alternative development strategies

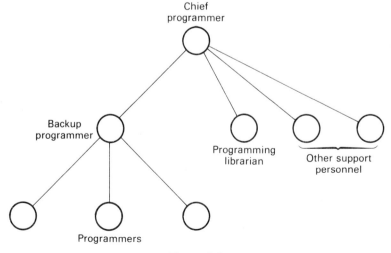

Figure 5.5

- participate in software design
- oversee program coding and testing

The programming librarian is responsible for maintaining the external and internal documentation libraries. The external library consists of documents such as source code, test data, system designs etc. The internal library serves as a backup in the event that information in the external library is lost.

5.7.2 Specialist teams

This project team organisation is a more restricted form of the chief programmer team approach in the sense that each member of the team has a special assignment to carry out. This approach takes advantage of the special skills that people may have and so a typical team will consist of:

- a chief programmer
- a backup programmer
- a documentation editor
- a project administrator
- a test specialist
- a software products (packages etc.) specialist
- a data administrator

5.7.3 Leaderless teams

This approach is not in widespread use although some feel that it has certain advantages. A leaderless team stays together for more than one project and has no *permanent* leader. A team member may rise to leadership on an informal basis depending on the nature of the project and the member's expertise. Work allocation between the members is done according to their knowledge and expertise.

5.8 Structured walkthroughs

The various deliverables produced at each stage of the development life-cycle need to be reviewed by the development personnel in order to gauge their correctness and effectiveness. A structured walkthrough is such a review which is carried out by staff at the same level.

A review session does not result in the correction of errors or changes in the deliverables. A structured walkthrough is a review session and not a repair session. Its purpose is to find areas where improvement can be made.

The review team must be large enough to have a meaningful discussion but not so large that nothing can be accomplished. Practice has shown that seven to nine members is the optimum number.

The team consists of at least the persons responsible for the project deliverable, a moderator who leads the review and a secretary who captures the details of the discussion.

As a general rule, management are not involved in a review session, since management is often associated with 'evaluation'. If management were to participate, the individuals responsible for the deliverable might feel pressurised to 'perfect' their product before the review session, which may result in unnecessary delays. On the other hand, managers may feel that if they raise any questions or identify mistakes, this would indicate that the work of the responsible individual is incompetent. Therefore, it is best to prepare and deliver a report to management about the points raised during the review rather than involving managers directly in the review itself.

Structured walkthroughs may be used at every stage of the development life-cycle.

During *requirements analysis*, a review will be carried out of the specification of functions, activities, data transactions, constraints etc. of the new system.

The *design review* concentrates on the design specification which should meet previously identified user requirements. The logical design in terms of structured charts, HIPO charts, data flow diagrams, entity relationship diagrams, report layouts etc. is communicated to the participants so that they can prepare for the review.

Code review concentrates on individual modules of a program. The produced code is compared with the original design in order to identify any deviations from it. Also, efficiency in execution, use of standard generic names for data etc. are considered during a code review. The purpose of this type of review is to try and discover which part of a program (or even design) needs to be modified so that the computer system will run more effectively. An early detection and subsequent correction of errors will greatly reduce maintenance costs when the system goes live.

5.9 Summary

Project management has been applied to engineering projects with some success and the experience and expertise gained has encouraged the development of a number of techniques to assist in this management. With regard to project planning and subsequent control, the most successful of these techniques has been network analysis. The generic term network analysis encompasses a number of specific theories which, in order to save terminology confusion, this chapter has grouped under the more commonly used name, PERT.

The PERT technique is based on the premise that a large project may be specified as a number of small, individual tasks, each being analysed in order to assign time-scales, costs, resources required and identify those that are predecessors of others. Engineering projects are conveniently simple to break down in this manner.

With the advances currently being experienced in the application of structured analysis and design methodologies to computer projects it might appear, at first glance, that the PERT technique would have an equal success in the planning and control of computer projects, as in the engineering world. However, while this structured approach to computer projects may assist in specifying a project as a number of tasks, the accurate estimation of time-scales and costs creates fundamental problems that require considerable research before the network analysis techniques can realise their full potential in the successful control of computer projects.

5.10 References

1. Levy, F., Thompson, G. and Weist, J. (1963). 'The ABCs of the Critical Path Method', *Harvard Business Review*, Oct.
2. Wooldridge, S. (1975). *Project Management in Data Processing*, Petrocelli/Charter.
3. Lock, D. (1984). *Project Management*, Gower.
4. Moore, P. and Thomas, H. (1976). *The Anatomy of Decisions*, Penguin.
5. Sommerville, I. (1985). *Software Engineering*, Addison Wesley.
6. Beech, C. and Burn, J. (1985). *Applications in Business Data Processing*, Pitman.
7. Burn, J. and O'Neil, M. (1986). *Information Analysis*, Pitman.
8. Saitow, A. (1969). 'CSPC: Reporting Project Progress to the Top', *Harvard Business Review*.
9. De Marco, T. (1978). *Structured Analysis and System Specification*, Yourdon.
10. Potts, D. (1982). 'Engineering Comes in from the Cold', *Engineering Computers*, Vol. 1, No. 5, Nov.
11. Mehrez, A. and Sinuary-Stern, Z. (1983). 'An Interactive Approach for Project Selection', *J. Oper. Res. Soc.*, Vol. 34, No. 7, July.
12. Gane, C. and Sarson, T. (1980). 'Structured Methodology: What have we learned?', *Computer World*, Sept.
13. Yourdon, C. and Constantine, L. (1978). *Structured Design*, Yourdon.
14. Jackson, M. (1983). *System Development*, Prentice-Hall.
15. Brooks, F. (1973). 'Mythical Man Months', *Datamation*, Dec.

Structured process analysis

6.1 Introduction

Before the introduction of structured techniques in the mid-1970s, systems generally tended to be badly developed. This resulted in system developments generally overrunning time and/or budget limits, systems that were very difficult and/or expensive to maintain and systems that invariably did not meet the goals or needs of users. These problems were caused through the inadequacies of the tools and techniques used. For example, techniques used tended to be quite empirical and intuitive, with little or no formalised discipline governing their use.

Because of these problems there has been a large amount of interest in the concepts and practice of structured techniques. Through their use, system development and maintenance is approached and carried through in a more disciplined and formal manner. If a complete structured methodology is taken towards system development and maintenance, then four disciplines are used. These are structured analysis, structured design, structured programming and top-down implementation. In theory, any one of the four can be used in system development although it is recommended that they be used together as they are highly compatible and supportive of each other.

6.1.1 Structured analysis

Structured analysis is a set of communication tools and guidelines for analysis which can be applied at any phase of system development or maintenance. The use of structured analysis is, however, especially effective in the analysis phase of system development and it is at this phase that its importance has been demonstrated.

The specifications, objectives and definitions of problems produced by structured analysis are more precise than the functional specification produced by classical tools and techniques. Another advantage of structured analysis is that its communication tools are graphical which facilitates communication with users and interested parties. The methodologies of structured analysis followed those of structured design and structured programming. It was from the tools and techniques of these two disciplines that structured analysis evolved.

6.1.2 Structured design

A large proportion of the cost of a system, over its life-cycle, is that of maintenance. Sixty-five per cent of the total expense of a system would not be an unusual figure to be spent on maintenance. Figures such as this are often regarded as an indication of bad design. Some of the problems of previous design packages involved communicating the principles of the design to the users, evaluating the design and its actual specification. One of the major problems was the tendency to rush in and produce a physical design before thoroughly understanding the logical design.

Structured design overcomes the above problems and also ensures the creation of a logical design before the physical design. A structured design is also much easier and cheaper to understand (and therefore change) than previous design methods. Furthermore, a feature of a structured approach to design is its graphical and concise documentation which enhances communication. Traditional design documentation consisted of large amounts of English narrative full of technical terms.

The first phase of structured design is to identify the flow of data in a system and the transformations carried out on it. These details can easily be obtained if structured analysis has been used since the details in question will appear on *data flow diagrams* and in the *data dictionary*. The next phase of structured design employs the use of transform analysis and transaction analysis to produce a structure chart. This is a hierarchical, modular design of the system in question and is the main tool of structured design. The production of a structure chart in itself is an interactive process with refinement and evaluation at each stage producing modifications which lead to a correct design. The next phases of structured design are evaluating/ refining the degree of coupling, the degree of cohesion, the shape of the modular structure, the span of control and the scope of effect. The final phase is packaging the design.

6.1.3 Structured programming

The theoretical reasoning behind structured programming is that any well-designed program is a combination of only the three structures: sequence, selection and repetition.[1]

It has been found that the quality of code produced by programmers using structured programming has increased greatly, although this quality is still difficult to measure. Programs written in structured code are more easily read and thus easier to understand and change. It is also generally believed that any inherent errors are easier to find and correct without much chance of other areas of a system having to be changed.

6.1.4 Top-down implementation

Top-down implementation is the technique whereby the top most modules in the hierarchy are tested first using stubs to replace lower-level ones. A stub is a very simplified version of the lower-level module in that its only function is to take and/or return values to the higher-level module as dictated by the design of the program. After the top-level modules have been tested and accepted as functioning correctly, the next level down are tested in conjunction with the high-level modules, again using stubs to replace still lower-level modules. This process is continued until the lowest-level modules have been tested and accepted as functioning correctly. As each level is added into the testing process, not all the modules at the level are necessarily added at once. What does happen is that one or more of the modules at the particular level are tested and then the others are added/ tested probably one by one.

A major advantage of the top-down implementation approach is that the important high-level interfaces are tested first. Another advantage is that modules can be coded and tested as the project proceeds. The importance of this latter point is that users can see some output and see the direction in which a system is proceeding before the system is in full production. Furthermore, if any changes are required, these can be accomplished without a major rewrite of a whole system. Top-down implementation is therefore less expensive than previous approaches to implementation in the long term since any problems can be trapped and solved at an early stage in the development life-cycle.

Two older approaches to implementation were to test all the modules together or to test all the bottom-level modules first using driver programs to emulate the higher-level ones. The problems with the first approach are that all the modules have to be written before testing can start properly and errors found in 'test all' are often difficult to locate. Once errors have been isolated, major parts of the system may have to be rewritten. In the second approach, which is known as a bottom-up approach, a major drawback is that as testing proceeds a problem can be found in a high-level interface which can result in a major part of the system having to be rewritten. A further disadvantage, compared to the top-down approach, is that driver programs are more complex than stubs and much more time-consuming to write.

6.1.5 Testing the design

A rigorous approach to the analysis and design of a system requires comprehensive testing at all stages. To assist in this problem the idea of the structured walkthrough was developed. A structured walkthrough is where members of a project team and users will check differing parts of systems design in order to locate and remove any errors. The principle of structured walkthrough is discussed in Section 5.8. There are various types of walkthroughs, some of which are analysis, design, code and test walkthroughs.

The purposes of analysis walkthroughs are to check the current physical model and the current logical model specifications. The people present at an analysis walkthrough would be the analyst, user representatives and perhaps a project programmer(s).

The design walkthrough is intended to validate the design for correctness and also to see that it concurs with the wishes of users. It is intended to locate errors and make changes before programming starts. The people present at such a walkthrough would be the analyst, systems designer, chief project programmer and perhaps other project programmers.

The people present at a code walkthrough would be the project programmers. The purpose of the code walkthrough is not only to check for correctness but also to familiarise each of the programmers with each other's work. The programmers will therefore obtain a view of the whole system and will also learn from other programmers; for example, they will gain from others' comments and suggested techniques.

The purpose of the test walkthrough is to check the sufficiency of test data. People present would be the analyst, project programmers, designer and perhaps an independent member of the organisation with specific responsibility for testing.

The overall advantage of walkthrough occurs in the early identification of errors or misunderstandings and their consequent correction. A further advantage is that it increases the project team's experience and understanding of the new system.

6.2 Traditional systems development

The traditional steps taken in the development of a new computer system are request evaluation, preliminary survey, feasibility study, detailed investigation and analysis, outline system design, detailed system design, programming, testing, documentation and implementation. Although testing and documentation are listed as separate stages, they should occur throughout the others.

If structured techniques are used in the development of a new computer system, then the steps taken may be similar to the above up to and including the first part of the analysis stage. The steps after the analysis stage are different in that outline design and detailed design are replaced by structured design. In the use of structured techniques the documentation produced, tools and methodology used are largely different to those in traditional techniques.

6.2.1 The analysis stage

The analyst(s) obtains information from feasibility documentation, detailed investigation, documentation and from the user area.

The analysis stage is, arguably, the most important of project development. Errors made at this stage will have greater repercussions on the system being developed than those made at other stages: they are far more expensive to rectify and may result in the failure of the new system in the extreme.

The purpose of the analysis stage is to study and thoroughly document the present functional system and to analyse the information requirements of the decision makers.

This includes documenting all data and information in use, where/when/how data is used, data likely to be used, present/possible problems, information/documentation extracted from the present system, information/documentation required from the proposed system and clearly specifying the objectives of the proposed information system. Analysis also has to ascertain if the proposed system is technically feasible and economically viable.

In order to arrive at a budget figure, the analysis stage may also produce documentation on various alternative information systems, performance figures, software proposals and data and information specifications.

One of the products of the analysis stage is the documentation of the requirements report which may involve some initial thoughts on the economics of possible hardware. However, this is not a rigid specification of how design should proceed, and many people believe that hardware should not be considered at all during analysis. One further product of the analysis stage may be a detailed plan for the project. This will show times when various activities should be completed and probably will also show times of various management meetings concerned with the project. The aspects of project management are dealt with in Chapter 5.

6.2.2 Functional specification

The purpose of the functional specification is to document all the aims and objectives which have to be achieved by the proposed system in order for it to satisfy the corporate information requirements. The equivalent of the functional specification in structured analysis is the structured specification.

One general difference between the functional specification and the structured specification is that the latter 'hardly acknowledges the existence of a computer. Instead it concentrates on the functions of the system in question.' These last two statements should become clearer in meaning later on in this chapter.

6.2.3 Analysis tools

One method of comparing the traditional approach with structured analysis is to list the tools and techniques used in the different approaches.

Classical tools

(1) *English narrative:* a large amount of the documentation from the analysis stage consists of English narrative.
(2) *Flow charts:* traditional flow charts are used to describe present and proposed procedures.

Structured analysis tools

(1) *Data flow diagrams (DFDs):* graphical picture of a system.
(2) *Data dictionary:* records information on processes, files and data.
(3) *Structured English:* logical English which is a mixture of English words and program type instructions such as IF and ELSE.
(4) *Decision tables:* a table showing conditions and actions related to a given part of a system or company policy.
(5) *Decision tree:* a tree-like structure showing decisions and actions.
(6) *Data access diagram:* schema showing the different access paths through stored data.

A detailed description of the traditional approach is beyond the scope of this book and the reader is referred elsewhere for further explanation.[6]

6.2.4 Analysis problems

Errors occurring at the analysis stage are more costly to rectify than those occurring at other stages of project development. The longer an error remains undetected, the greater the cost will be to rectify it. The remainder of this section describes some of the whys and wherefores of analysis errors.

User co-operation

An essential element of the analysis stage is user participation and co-operation. Without this, a new information system is doomed to failure. The analyst needs the user's help in order to document the present system, to derive the specifications of the proposed system and to gain the required feedback as the project progresses. The term feedback refers to the users checking the analyst's findings, informing him of any errors in the documentation and of any changes in the requirements as the project is proceeding.

Reasons why an analyst may have problems in getting user co-operation are the users' concern over job security and about having their particular work investigated, attitudes of the trade unions and the shortcomings in the analysis tools used. An analyst may experience difficulty obtaining co-operation from management and other workers in the analysis area due to resistance to change. This can take many forms and occurs when people feel that they have not been considered or consulted enough about the change. They may feel that the change is being thrust upon them. A change in the system is often a technical one which results in changes in working locations, job practice and human relationships. Further problems occur because a change in a system may cause changes in management authority. There are potentially great problems if the system being changed crosses organisational boundaries since job demarcations and responsibilities become affected and this may result in hostility. While some of these problems could be resolved by higher management, the analyst cannot ignore them and should do his best to resolve each particular type that may exist. For example, if people feel they have not been consulted enough, then meetings of all concerned should be set up, communication lines opened and users encouraged to be actively involved in the project.

The tools of structured analysis are designed to ease the communication between the analyst and the user by providing unambiguous expressions of the findings and proposals which result during the analysis phase.

Use of classical tools

The two main classical tools used to produce the functional specification and to document the user area in question are English narrative and flow charts. The documents so produced from the analysis stage tend to be large in volume and difficult to read.

The problems in using English narrative are that it makes the functional specification excessively large, it can disguise important points, it can hide oversights and contains a lot of redundancy which causes great difficulty for users to comprehend what the new system will be like. Even if the functional specification could be supplemented by summaries or précis, the user could still be intimidated by the sheer size of the full specification.

The problem of using flow charts is that due to the symbols used in constructing them, aspects of the *physical* design of the new system are specified, for example, disc or tape filing. This is not an analysis task but a design stage task. Another problem with flow charts is that they are difficult to maintain and hard to follow, especially if they extend over several pages.

Partitioning

In the majority of cases where a system is to be analysed, it is necessary to partition, which means to segment the system into smaller pieces to be analysed. A top-down approach involves the process of breaking down a large complex problem into smaller less complicated ones. Then each of the smaller problems are broken into even smaller problems. The process of breaking down is continued until problems are small enough to be clearly defined and managed. An advantage of this approach is that each of the pieces of the larger problem can be organised back together to form the whole without much difficulty. Another advantage is that not only are the components of a system specified but also the major interfaces between them are defined. In the top-down approach, the major interfaces at the top can be tested early on in the project life-cycle and any problems found can be resolved. In contrast to this, the old bottom-up approach would not find bugs with the top-level interfaces until later on in the project, which could well result in vast areas of a system being rewritten or re-analysed. Perhaps the greatest advantage of the top-down approach is that an outline of a system can be shown to the user early on before anyone has wasted time working from hazy specifications.

In that structured analysis is a top-down approach, it enables easy partitioning of a system and also easier analysis/documentation of a particular area of it. If classical methodology is used, then it tends to lean towards a bottom-up approach and it is difficult to organise segments back into the whole system or to relate them to each other.

This is because the bottom-up approach starts with what may be the smallest parts of the system, but these pieces have ill-defined boundaries and may overlap. The net result is that it is difficult to analyse a small area as a separate part. Also, as analysis proceeds it may be found on nearing the top that there is a major factor which cannot be ignored and causes a large amount of the previous analysis to be redundant.

Maintenance

As analysis proceeds new facts, figures and changes are encountered and documentation has to be maintained. Using traditional tools, this can require a lot of rewriting and checking which can be a mammoth task in itself. One of the reasons for this is that if there is a change, it is not always clear which other areas are affected if a bottom-up approach has been used. Structured analysis is a top-down approach and maintenance is much easier since it is much clearer which areas are affected by a change.

One of the worst aspects of maintenance in systems development lies with that of the functional specification. Because of the sheer bulk and complexity of the functional specification, its maintenance proved very difficult under the traditional approach. This often meant that once the functional specification had been written and passed, that was the way the system was developed and virtually all changes were ignored. This is obviously wrong as the implemented system will not reflect the user's current and future information requirements. Through the use of structured techniques, the structured specification is more easily maintained.

A further problem is that system development may take a very long time and changes in the requirements can occur before it has been completely specified. One cause of change can be due to a user's increased understanding of his needs as a system develops. Another cause could be due to organisational changes such as the dispersal of a department so more or less is required of the system. Changes may be caused by government legislation such as greater privacy control of data as in the Data Protection Act of 1984. Another cause of change may be due to previous communication between the analyst and the user.

In the development of a system, change should be accepted as inevitable. The further into the development a change request occurs, the greater the likely cost of implementing it. So all changes should be evaluated on cost/benefit grounds and a decision should be taken by users and analysts on whether or not to implement them.

The rest of this chapter discusses the techniques and tools used in structured analysis.

6.3 Data flow diagrams

A data flow diagram (DFD) is a pictorial representation of a system. As such it is a model which shows the route through which the system's data travels. This system's model (that is, DFD) is developed in a top-down fashion. The system is partitioned by levelling DFDs, where a successive level of a DFD shows more detail than the previous level. Decomposition of the DFD continues until a point is reached where it is impossible to go any further or it is pointless to continue.

The main advantages of data flow diagrams are:

(1) They are graphical ('A picture says a thousand words').
(2) They greatly help in partitioning.

(3) Their structure is such that once a system has been documented, any particular part of it can be looked at with ease, its place in the system easily derived, and all interfaces to/from/in the part can be seen.
(4) They enhance user communication.
(5) They concentrate on flow of data through the system.
(6) They place little stress on control information such as who/what decides and acts when.
(7) They reduce the volume of the functional specification.
(8) They minimise documentation of processes.

6.3.1 Data flow diagram example

Shown in Figure 6.1 is an example of a data flow diagram which contains the four symbols used in the drawing of a data flow chart.

The situation presented is an envisaged part of a publisher's system where a bookshop will request a quantity of books to be despatched. The diagram shows that the area under study is restricted to verifying whether an order can be met; not shown are the various error paths possible.

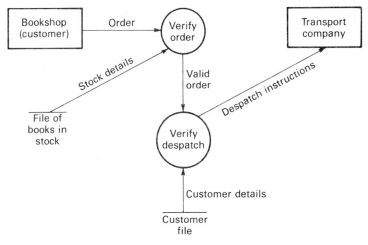

Figure 6.1

6.3.2 Constituents of DFDs

The four constituents of a DFD are a named vector (data flow), a square (origin or destination of data to and from a system), a straight line (a store of data known as a file) and a circle (process which transforms data).

Other naming conventions that are used are where a process is represented by an upright rectangle with rounded corners and a file is represented by two parallel lines joined at one end. This type of convention may be seen in Gane and Sarson.[2] Further conventions are used where a process is represented by an oval or a square.

Origin/destination of data

The origin of data entering a system is known as a source and the destination of data leaving the system is known as a sink. A source may also be a sink. Examples of what might be a source or sink are an author, another system or customers.

A source or sink on a DFD is represented by a named square: the name appears inside it. To see how the above examples would be represented on a DFD, refer to Figure 6.2. The source/sink labelled 'Production' is the name of another system.

| Author | | Production | | Customers |

Figure 6.2

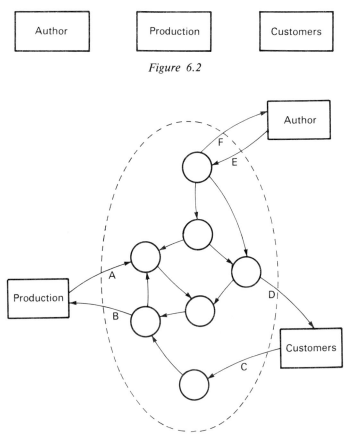

Figure 6.3

Sources and sinks lie outside the area being analysed. They are not analysed to find what processes, data flow or files they contain. However, the area under study may need to include analysis of a source(s) or sink(s) as analysis proceeds. If this happens, then new sources and sinks will be created. The opposite is also true where the area under analysis may contract again, creating new sources and sinks.

Major benefits of showing sources and sinks are that the boundary of the area under analysis is clearly defined and the data entering and leaving the system (the interface) is specified (see Figure 6.3). It can be seen from Figure 6.3 that the area under study is enclosed by a black dotted line. The data flows entering the system are A, E and C; those leaving the system are B, D and F. The diagram also shows that 'Authors', 'Customers' and 'Production' are both a source and a sink.

Data flow

A data flow on a DFD is shown as a named vector. The best conceptual way of thinking about a data flow is as a tube down which a flow of data is sent in the direction of the arrow. With the exception of a small number of cases, each data flow has to be given a name which describes the data it contains. The name chosen should be such that it is clear to the user what it represents when he looks at a DFD. Two other important points on the name chosen are that it should be unique and should be entered into a data dictionary together with a description of its structure.

It can be seen from Figure 6.1 that sources/sinks, data flows, transforms and files are all given descriptive names. Some method is needed to store details of these four elements as a necessary part of systems documentation and as an aid to the systems analyst(s).

For example, the data flow known as 'Despatch instruction' in Figure 6.1 may have a structure as shown below:

Despatch instruction
Customer — Name
Customer — Address
Customer — Number
Book   — Title
Book   — Quantity
Order   — Amount

An entry would also be made in the data dictionary, in alphabetical order, for each of the above data-structure elements. Together with each entry, such details as the elements' field size and type should be held. Other details about the data flow such as source, destination and frequency should be held.

The data dictionary is therefore essential as documentation and as a reference tool.

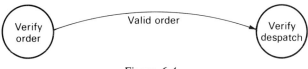

Figure 6.4

On any data flow there should not be two bundles of different data travelling along it. To illustrate this, refer to Figure 6.4. The data flow Valid order could consist of the request from the bookshop plus another internal form which might contain an internal customer number for the bookshop, data as to whether it was a repeat order and perhaps some sort of priority data. The two forms are one bundle of data and therefore can travel along the same data flow.

An example of where two data flows should be used between transforms and not one is as shown in Figure 6.5. The situation shown is one where an accounts process produces payments to an author. An advance payment for a new book will be a rare occurrence but will be required in certain instances. Royalty payments should, however, occur on a more regular basis.

There are two different data flows as the two sets of data do not form one bundle of data. The two different bundles serve separate purposes and in most cases, as a rule, have little in common.

This type of situation and the fact that two different bundles of data should not travel along the same data flow are important points in drawing DFDs.

Another point about data flows is that they should not cross and, except on rare occasions, it should be possible to achieve this. When it is necessary to cross data flows, they can be documented as shown on Figure 6.6.

Two other important aspects about data flows are that they are not flows of control or initialisations of processes. An indicator of control information is where a data flow enters a transform but has nothing to do with resultant data flow.

Examples of control flows or initiators are 'Fetch record', 'Process Friday' and 'Start if total correct'. The examples just stated could probably be found on a flow chart but not on a DFD since it is not a flow chart in the traditional sense. A DFD does not show the order in which things are done but shows the ways data moves through a system and how it is transformed; it is a logical representation of data.

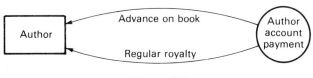

Figure 6.5

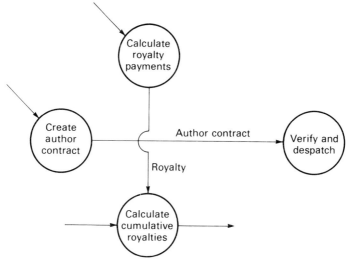

Figure 6.6

Transform (process)

A transform is also known as a process and in the naming convention it is represented by a circle. As stated before, a process transforms data flows passed to it to give the data or information flows leaving it.

Each transform is given a name, which should explain its function, and a number. The number given to a transform is dependent on levelling. A brief description of levelling DFDs follows although a fuller description can be found in 'Levelling of data flow diagrams' (Section 6.6).

The top-level (first-level) DFD of a system being analysed gives an overview of the whole system. The border of the system, net input/output data flows and sources/sinks can be seen. The transforms which appear at the top level are numbered consecutively 1, 2, 3, 4 etc. (see Figure 6.7). Each of the transforms on the top-level DFD, known as the parent diagram, are examined to see what transforms, data flows and possible files they consist of. A 'child' diagram (lower-level DFD) is then drawn for each of the transforms, on the top level, that can be further partitioned. Examples of this can be seen on Figures 6.8 and 6.9. On Figure 6.8 the partitioning of transform 1 from the parent diagram is shown and on Figure 6.9 the partitioning of transform 3 from the parent diagram is shown.

Every transform on each of the child diagrams is given a number depending upon which transform is being shown in greater detail. For example, in Figure 6.9, each of the consecutively numbered transforms have the prefix 3 which indicates that they are breakdowns of transform 3 from the top-level diagram.

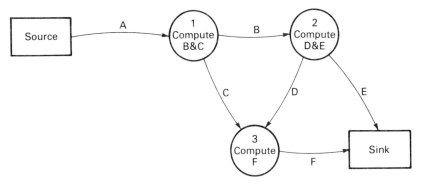

Figure 6.7 Top-level DFD (diagram 0)

If any of the transforms on the child diagrams can themselves be further partitioned, then we would draw a third-level DFD. For example, say transform 3.2 on Figure 6.10 could be broken down into five transforms, then a third-level DFD would be drawn where they would all have the prefix 3.2, that is, 3.2.1, 3.2.2, 3.2.3, 3.2.4 and 3.2.5.

The process of levelling is continued on every transform until we obtain functional primitives, which are transforms small enough to be described in about a page of text, although this stopping point is merely a guide and not a 'golden rule'.

As stated before, the name given to a transform should convey its func-

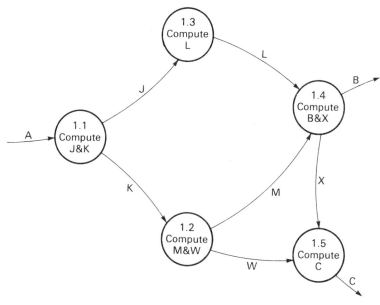

Figure 6.8 Second-level DFD (diagram 1)

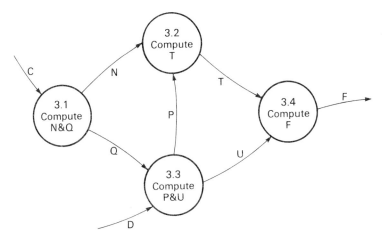

Figure 6.9 Second-level DFD (diagram 3)

tion. This enhances clarity of DFDs, readability and also user communication.

Other points that should be borne in mind when naming a process are:

(1) The name given should be unambiguous.
(2) The name given should be distinct from all other names given to transforms.
(3) Names with physical implications such as 'Search' should not be included. (The term 'Search' has implementation connotations.)
(4) The name given should describe all the functions of a process.
(5) If great difficulty is found in naming a process, then this may be a sign of bad partitioning. The solution to this is to go back and repartition.

There are cases where transforms may not transform data in the physical sense but do so in a logical sense. This type occurs when an incoming data flow consists of two or more data flows and the transform distributes the individual ones. An example of this can be seen in Figure 6.10 where the process, Direct transaction, routes the various incoming transactions from customers.

It can be seen that the process has not physically transformed the data flows in any manner but has merely logically transformed the data in that our comprehension of it has been changed.

In such a situation (as shown in Figure 6.10) cluttering of the DFD can be avoided by grouping all the incoming transactions into one data flow as shown in Figure 6.11. In general, the name given to the grouped data flow may well be found to be not very meaningful. However, this problem is resolved in that a full description of the data flow will be found in the data dictionary with a description of its contents.

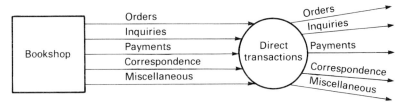

Figure 6.10

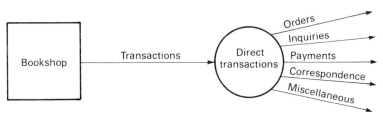

Figure 6.11

At some stage, information about a process such as its name, number, inputs, outputs, files/data bases it accesses and logic (policy by which a process transforms data flow) have to be recorded. To accomplish this, the data dictionary is used.

In the case of a manual data dictionary being used, there will probably not be space to hold the entire process logic. The solution would then be to produce a summary of the process logic in the data dictionary and a detailed account of it on a separate document. This separate document is attached to the relevant process entry in the data dictionary and is often referred to as a mini spec.[4]

As process logic can be very complex, some method of representing it pictorially and recording it in an unambiguous fashion is required. The recording tools used in structured analysis are structured English, decision tables and decision trees.

Transform and procedural association of data flows

Situations sometimes arise in which the procedural association between a transform and its data flows may be depicted on a DFD. For example:

(1) If it is not clear which of the input data flows the transform requires in order to be able to carry out its function.

(2) If it is not apparent what combination of output data flows the transform must produce.

Figure 6.12

The convention used to depict the procedural relationships is as follows:

* represents a logical AND of data flows
⊕ represents a logical exclusive OR of data flows
0 represents a logical inclusive OR of data flows

An example of the nomenclature can be seen in Figure 6.12 which depicts another of the functions of a publisher. The situation envisaged is one where synopsis for books are judged against information on potential sales for different types of book.

It can be seen that both incoming data flows, synopsis and market information are needed by the transform in order for it to output either, but not both, contract or refusal letter. The data flow market information on Figure 6.12 represents an analysis which may consist of many subject areas of books.

If the situation shown on Figure 6.12 is now expanded to one where authors can now submit synopsis sample chapter(s) or the complete manuscript, then the resultant DFD is shown as Figure 6.13. The diagram shows that market information and some combination of synopsis, sample chapter, manuscript is needed in order for the transform to carry out its function. By some combination, what is meant is that all three author items, any two of the three, of just one of the items will be required.

The use of procedural annotation can lead to ambiguity in the interpretation of DFDs. For example, in Figure 6.14 the transform requires both data flows A and E in order to carry out its function. If certain conditions are met by A and E, then the transform outputs data flows B and C. If certain conditions are not met by A and E, then the transform outputs data flow D alone. However, Figure 6.14 is ambiguous in that it could be interpreted

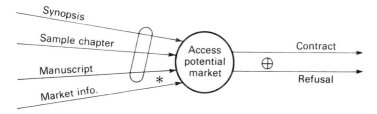

Figure 6.13

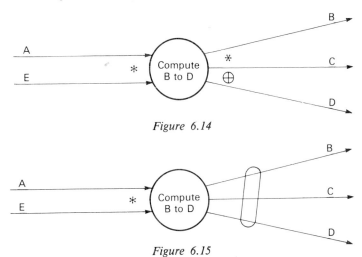

Figure 6.14

Figure 6.15

by someone as meaning that B and C are output or B and D are output. An even more ambiguous representation of Figure 6.14 is shown in Figure 6.15.

The ambiguity of situations such as depicted in Figures 6.14 and 6.15 can be overcome by splitting data flows as shown in Figure 6.16.

Showing procedural annotation on a DFD is depicting control considerations which is not really its function. (A DFD shows flow and transformation of data in a system.) Control considerations are documented in a mini-specification which is written for every process, but they may also arise in the functional partitioning of DFDs. Other arguments against annotating procedural aspects are that it tends to clutter up DFDs and when it is used

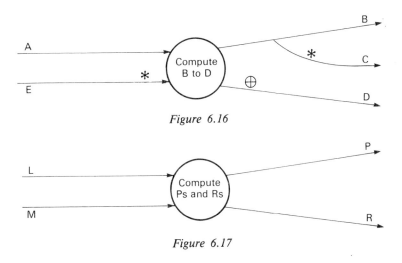

Figure 6.16

Figure 6.17

the analysts tend to dream up more and more complicated procedural connections.

However, it is thought by Weinberg[4] that the showing of procedural associations at about the primitive DFD level may be useful for certain users. For example, system designers are concerned with fine detail and may find it useful to tell at a glance what control considerations are necessary.

Finally, procedural annotation does not show the relationship of input data flows to output data flows. An example of this is shown in Figure 6.17. The transform in question does two different things: it appears to transform Ds to Ps and Ms to Rs, although this may not be exactly what was intended.

File

A file on a DFD is a point where data is temporarily stored and is represented by a named straight line. The name given to a file should be unique as this will be stored in the data dictionary along with other details about the file, for example, the data structures it contains. The name given to a file should also be such that users easily recognise what it represents and should describe the contents in an unambiguous manner. The fact that a file has a unique name does not mean it cannot appear on the same DFD more than once. This may be necessary to avoid lines crossing and excessive complexity of the DFD.

A few examples of what might merit as a file are a folder, a notebook, a magnetic disk or tape, a data base, a safe, a catalogue, or a filing cabinet. If data is stored in any of these, then the place in question may be regarded as a file.

Data may be read from (see Figure 6.18) or placed in (see Figure 6.19) a file. As can be seen, if data is taken from a file, then there is a data flow from the file; or if data is placed in a file, then there is a data flow to the file. The situation depicted in Figures 6.18 and 6.19 is that of a publisher. In Figure 6.18 incoming orders for books are arriving at the process 'Verify order'. The process in question reads the books in stock file to verify that the order can be satisfied. In Figure 6.19 the 'Valid order' data from Figure

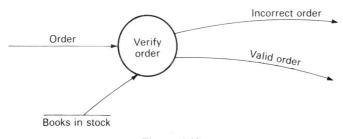

Figure 6.18

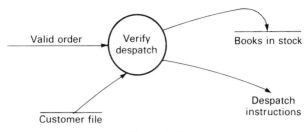

Figure 6.19

6.18 is matched with customer file details and if the customer details are correct a despatch instruction is generated.

If the same type of data is both placed on and read from a file by a process, then this is represented by a single data flow having an arrow head at either end (see Figure 6.20). However, if different data is travelling to and from a file to a process, then the two data flows should be shown (see Figure 6.21). This is possible as a file may consist of several different data elements/records.

It should be noted that if data is read from a file only in order to do an output to the same file, then only the data flow to the file is shown (see Figure 6.22). This is an important point to bear in mind when drawing DFDs. As a rule it can be stated that only the overall data flow to and from a file is shown.

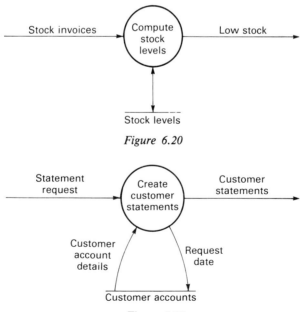

Figure 6.20

Figure 6.21

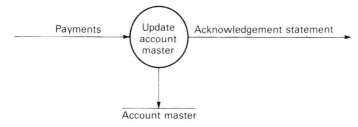

Figure 6.22

It can be seen from Figure 6.22 that in order to update the Account master file it would have to be read first. However, the file is only read in order to write to it. The data read from the file is not used for any outgoing data flow from the process except back to the file itself. Thus the overall data flow is to the file.

Why it is important to follow this convention is shown in Figure 6.23. It can be seen that there is a file called Authors which only has data flows as shown. This means that the file is only ever written to and is never used by anyone. This is an indication that an error has been made either in information gathering from users or in drawing the DFD. It can be seen that if a data flow was shown going from the file to a process, for the purpose of a simple update, this type of error could easily be overlooked.

Sometimes it is useful to show any search parameters passed to a file. This is true in the design stage and if access is being made to a database. The search parameter passed by the process to the file or database is written alongside the data flow and has an arrow head to show that it is a search parameter being passed by the process. This can be seen in Figure 6.24.

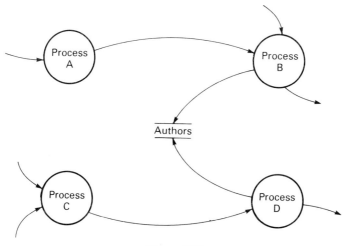

Figure 6.23

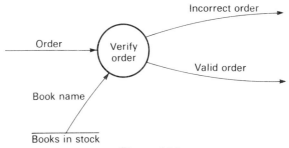

Figure 6.24

6.4 The data dictionary (DD)

A data dictionary (DD) is a repository of data about data.

Without a DD the DFDs are just pretty pictures that give some idea of what is going on in a system. It is only when each and every level of the DFD has been rigorously defined that the whole can constitute a specification. The set of rigorous definitions of all DFD elements is the DD.

There is one DD entry of each unique data flow that appears anywhere in the DFD set. There is one DD entry for each functional primitive in the set.

Thus the definitions of the following appear in the DD:

● data flow
● file
● process
● data element

A data element is a special kind of data flow, one that cannot be decomposed into subordinate data flows.

Definitions of the DD are top-down partitioning of data. If we know that the data flow A is composed of one B and one C and that B is made up of B1, B2 and B3, while C is always C1 and C2, we could write the definitions as

A = B1 + B2 + B3 + C1 + C2

If a flow is complex, it makes sense to define it in terms of meaningful high-level subordinates and then define those subordinates.

Definition of data and processes use the following tools:

(1) Data flows, data elements and files are defined by using relational operators

= equivalent to
+ AND
[ ] EITHER OR (components separated by /)
{ } ITERATIONS of the enclosed components
( ) enclosed component is OPTIONAL

DATA FLOW NAME: ORDER
ALIASES : NONE

COMPOSITION : Order-no. + Customer-no. + Customer-name +

$^4_1$ $\left\{ \text{Order details} \right\}$

NOTES :

.

.

.

FILE NAME : BOOK FILE
ALIASES : NONE

COMPOSITION : ISBN + Author-name + Author-initials + Book-title +
Subject-class + ···

.

.

.

PROCESS NAME : CALCULATE DISCOUNT
PROCESS NUMBER: 5.6.2.3.

PROCESS DESCRIPTION:

If CUST-LOCATION is over FAR-EAST

.

.

.

If CUST-STANDING is over 2 years
Set discount 35%

Figure 6.25

(2) Functional primitives are defined by using structured English, decision trees and decision tables.

A DD entry might include:

Customer order = Order-no. + Customer-no. + Customer-name +

$^4_1$ {Order details}

+ Total

Order details = Author + Title + ISBN + Qty + Price

A typical DD layout might be as shown in Figure 6.25.

6.5 Recording process logic

Although DFDs depict all the data flows and transforms in a system, some method of recording exactly what goes on inside a transform is required.

In considering what tools to use in order to achieve this it is important to consider the people that will have to view or use this documentation. The people so concerned are users, analysts, designers and programmers.

The traditional tools used to describe process logic are English narrative and flow charts. The inherent problems with English narrative, as already mentioned, are that it is lengthy and likely to contain omissions, contradictions and ambiguities. Its use to describe process logic is a potential source of mis-interpretation and error. This is particularly true if processing logic is at all complex. In a situation such as this, programmers may spend a great amount of time trying to fathom out and rewrite specifications.

One of the problems of using flow charts is that they will probably be totally meaningless to users and therefore useless to obtain assurances that the documentation is a true representation of the present system or that the specification is acceptable to the user.

The tools used in structured analysis to describe a process are decision tables, decision trees and structured English.

6.5.1 Structured English

Structured English is a sub-set of the English language adopted to follow the theoretical structure of structured programming. Structured programming techniques adopt the axiom that any well-designed program is a combination of only the three structures: sequence, selection and repetition. (This was first argued by Dijkstra in 1972 whose work was based on that of Bohm and Jacopini.[5] It was further argued by Dijkstra that branching by GO TO instructions creates unsound structures that are prone to error.) Sequence refers to the normal sequential execution of simple program constructions. Selection is a decision structure such as IF THEN ELSE. Repetition is a loop statement such as DO WHILE, REPEAT UNTIL or PERFORM UNTIL. In a similar manner, process logic is described by structured English by declarative statements, decision statements and repetition statements.

In order to avoid the problems of English narrative, structured English follows certain guidelines which are:

(1) Nouns used should be documented in the data dictionary.
(2) Little if any punctuation is used.
(3) Statements should be concise.
(4) Each declarative statement (imperative statement) should contain a verb which expresses the function.
(5) A small set of logic statements such as IF ELSE are used.
(6) Adjectives such as quicker, less, better, splendid, worse and excellent are used as little as possible.

An example of some structured English statements is shown in Figure

Enter CUSTOMER-NAME and CUSTOMER-ADDRESS on BILL

Enter CUSTOMER-AMOUNT-DUE on BILL

Calculate CUSTOMER-DISCOUNT

Enter CUSTOMER-DISCOUNT on BILL

Calculate GROSS-AMOUNT-DUE

Enter GROSS-AMOUNT-DUE on BILL

File BILL in BILL-FILE

Figure 6.26

6.26. The situation imagined is part of a billing process. The names which appear in capital letters on the figure are terms which are defined in the data dictionary. It can be seen that almost no punctuation is used, all the statements are concise, all the verbs clearly express the required function, the use of adjectives is totally absent and all nouns are defined in the data dictionary.

Decision statements in structured English can be represented by the IF ELSE construct which is equivalent to the IF THEN ELSE construct of structured programming. Another which is used is the IF THEN OTHERWISE construct. For an example of the IF ELSE construct, see Figure 6.27. It can be seen that indentation has been used. This is to enhance readability by making it clear which ELSE belongs to which IF. It can also be seen on Figure 6.27 that IF ELSE statements have been joined by dotted lines: this makes logic easier to follow. A further point on Figure 6.27 is that it could have been written as an IF THEN OTHERWISE CONSTRUCT but would have been much more complex.

The main concern in using structured English is that logic should be easy to follow and that it should be easy to read. If this is not the case, then it is permissible to slacken the guidelines governing structured English and include extra words. It has to be remembered that many users, unlike

IF CUSTOMER is from FAR-EAST

  ·   IF CUSTOMER is over 2 years standing
  ·
  ·   ·   Set DISCOUNT 35%
  ·
  ·   ELSE (CUSTOMER 2 years or less standing)
  ·
  ·   Set DISCOUNT 25%
  ·

ELSE (CUSTOMER not from FAR-EAST)

    Set DISCOUNT 15%

Figure 6.27

Policy for insurance discount

IF CLIENT is under 25 years old
·
·   IF CLIENT has had under 2 CLAIMS
·   ·
·   · Award CLIENT 15% DISCOUNT
·   ·
·   ELSE (CLIENT has had over 2 CLAIMS)
·
·   Award CLIENT 5% DISCOUNT
·
ELSE (CLIENT is over 25 years old)
·
·   IF CLIENT has had under 2 CLAIMS
·   ·
·   · Award CLIENT 30% DISCOUNT
·   ·
ELSE (CLIENT has had over 1 CLAIMS)
·
·   Award CLIENT 10% DISCOUNT

Figure 6.28

programmers, will not be familiar with logic constructs such as IF THEN ELSE. If it is found using structured English that many IF ELSE constructs are required and that logic is not easy to follow, then there are several courses of action that can be taken. The first of these is to include extra English words. Another is to use a logical AND to combine conditions and thus reduce indentation. In using compound conditions it is permissible to use ORs. However ANDs and ORs should never be used together as this will make difficult reading.

The CASE construct is used in situations where there are many possible courses of action but only one applies. For an example of this, see Figure

Policy governing orders of goods

CASE 1 (New customer)

Send CUSTOMER-DETAILS-FORM

Send REQUEST-FOR-PAYMENT

CASE 2 (Old customer behind on payments)

Send BILL

Save BOOKS-ORDER

CASE 3 (Old customer not behind on payments)

Send GOODS

Send INVOICE

Figure 6.29

6.29. It can be seen that there are three possible situations which can occur but only one of which will be applicable for any one order. Thus in using a CASE construct the CASE which is relevant is applied, and the next part of the policy applied is that following the CASE construct.

Repetition (iteration) of statements in structured English is normally achieved through the use of DO-WHILE or REPEAT-UNTIL constructs. An example of the REPEAT-UNTIL construct can be seen in Figure 6.30 where for every customer account the actions described by the imperative statements between IF and ELSE are carried out or the action described by the statement following ELSE is carried out.

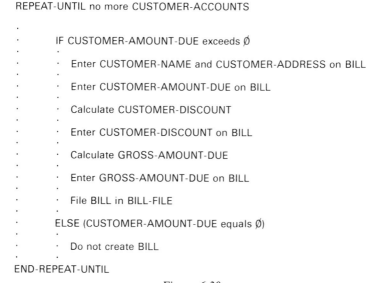

```
REPEAT-UNTIL no more CUSTOMER-ACCOUNTS
    ·
    ·        IF CUSTOMER-AMOUNT-DUE exceeds Ø
    ·        ·
    ·        ·   Enter CUSTOMER-NAME and CUSTOMER-ADDRESS on BILL
    ·        ·
    ·        ·   Enter CUSTOMER-AMOUNT-DUE on BILL
    ·        ·
    ·        ·   Calculate CUSTOMER-DISCOUNT
    ·        ·
    ·        ·   Enter CUSTOMER-DISCOUNT on BILL
    ·        ·
    ·        ·   Calculate GROSS-AMOUNT-DUE
    ·        ·
    ·        ·   Enter GROSS-AMOUNT-DUE on BILL
    ·        ·
    ·        ·   File BILL in BILL-FILE
    ·        ·
    ·        ELSE (CUSTOMER-AMOUNT-DUE equals Ø)
    ·        ·
    ·        ·   Do not create BILL
    ·        ·
END-REPEAT-UNTIL
```

Figure 6.30

6.5.2 Decision tables

Decision tables are useful in cases where a decision problem contains many sets of conditions which can occur and as a result many possible actions. The particular action which is taken depends upon which set of conditions prevails. The advantage of a decision table over structured English in such situations is that a decision table shows the policy in a neat condensed format. Furthermore, if there has been any ambiguity or omissions in the policy description, these will become apparent in the decision table. The decision table is therefore useful to an analyst in checking his understanding of a policy and checking this for correctness with the user. Decision tables are also useful descriptions of policy to programmers as time will be saved through programmers not having to spend time checking that their understanding of the policy is correct. They are also useful for describing specifications as analysts again can check for ambiguities or omissions.

After calculating the number of rules, all the possible actions should be identified. The next step to be taken is to decide which values should be placed under the rules and opposite the decisions. The best way of doing this is to take each of the decisions in turn and fill in its row of values before proceeding to the next decision. Figure 6.31 illustrates a decision table. There are occasions when a decision table might involve a large number

	Rules												
	1	2	3	4	5	6	7	8	9	10	11	12	13
Conditions													
New customer	Y	Y	Y	—	—	—	—	—	—	—	—	—	—
				A									
1-5 yrs custm	—	—	—	Y	Y	Y	—	—	—	—	—	—	—
				N									
5-10 yrs custm	—	—	—	—	—	—	Y	Y	Y	—	—	—	—
				Y									
10+ yrs custm	—	—	—	—	—	—	—	—	—	—	Y	Y	Y
Credit good	Y	Y	Y	N	Y	Y	Y	Y	Y	Y	Y	Y	Y
Size order:													
5-10	Y	—	—	Y	—	—	Y	—	—	Y	—	—	—
				A									
10-20	—	Y	—	—	Y	—	—	Y	—	—	Y	—	—
				N									
20+	—	—	Y	—	—	Y	—	—	Y	—	—	Y	Y
				Y									
Actions													
Discount of:													
5%	X	—	—	—	—	—	—	—	—	—	—	—	—
10%	—	X	—	—	X	—	—	—	—	—	—	—	—
15%	—	—	X	—	—	·X	—	X	—	—	—	—	—
20%	—	—	—	—	—	—	X	—	X	—	X	—	—
25%	—	—	—	—	—	—	—	—	—	X	—	X	—
35%	—	—	—	—	—	—	—	—	—	—	—	—	X
Pre payment request:	—	—	—	X	—	—	—	—	—	—	—	—	—

Key:
custm = custom
yrs = years

Y = yes
N = no
X = action to be taken

Figure 6.31 Decision table for customer discounts

of rules, say 96 for example. The resulting decision table will be too large to be drawn on one sheet of paper. An approach taken to this problem is to draw portions on different sheets of paper. Another approach taken is to group conditions which result in the same action and redefine the group of conditions which will result in an overall decrease in the size of the table. A problem with this second approach is that the decision table will be difficult to maintain in the future as actions change for a rule of conditions.

6.5.3 Decision trees

Decision trees are an alternative means of graphically representing the information shown in a decision table. A decision tree is similar to a decision table in that all conditions/actions are shown and is an easy method of checking that all possible conditions/actions are present.

Two advantages decision trees have over decision tables are they are much simpler to draw and are much more easily understood by users. For example, if a programmer was asked to draw a decision table, then in a lot of cases he would have difficulty. However, if a programmer, or other such work-orientated person, were asked to draw a decision tree he would have much less difficulty since top-down programming methodology follows a similar procedure. One reason put forward by De Marco[3] why users and other people have very little difficulty in understanding decision trees is that most people are familiar with the tree concept form having seen family trees at one time or another.

Another advantage is that it is much easier to answer a question from a decision tree than it is from a decision table.

6.6 Levelling of data flow diagrams

In Section 6.3 of this chapter, a description of the concept of levelling was given. There were, however, several points overlooked. One of these is that through the process of levelling, details are successively refined, until functional primitives are reached, without ever presenting too much detail at once. A second overall point about levelling is that, unlike flow charts, a levelled set of DFDs is easily updated.

6.6.1 Context diagram

The context diagram is conceptually one level above the top-level DFD. It consists of one transform with data flows which represents the net inputs and outputs of the area under study. An example of a context diagram can be seen in Figure 6.32.

The data flows to and from the transform on a context diagram are in fact the method by which the boundary of the area under study is defined.

Figure 6.32 Context diagram

Also, it should be noted that the name given to the transform should describe the area under study but is likely not to be a description of everything happening in that area.

6.6.2 Diagram numbering

The top-level DFD is labelled diagram 0. Also, if any of the transforms on the top-level DFD can be partitioned, then another diagram is drawn depicting the transforms which make up the top-level transform. The number given to these child diagrams is the number of the transforms it is showing in greater detail. For example, the child diagram of transform 1 would be labelled diagram 1, that of transform 2 would be labelled diagram 2 and so on. This is the convention which is followed throughout the levelled set of DFDs. To further clarify this, suppose there was a transform 3.2.4.1 which could be further partitioned. The child diagram drawn for this transform would be labelled diagram 3.2.4.1.

6.6.3 Process numbering

Each process is consecutively numbered from 1 upwards and is given the prefix of the process it is showing in greater detail. As can be imagined, numbers may become too long to fit inside a transform or could have the effect of cluttering up a DFD. In this type of situation the prefix is dropped and the transforms are numbered .1, .2, .3 etc. It is not important that the prefix has been dropped as this can be ascertained from the diagram number on the DFD. For an example of this, see Figure 6.33.

6.6.4 Corresponding inputs and outputs

If a transform is partitioned, then the net inputs on the child diagram must directly correspond to those on the parent transform. For example, referring back to Figure 6.7 it can be seen that transform 1 has input/output data flow A, B and C. Referring to Figure 6.8, the child diagram of transform 1, it can be seen that the diagram also has net input/output data flow A, B and C.

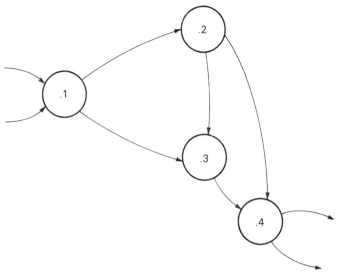

Figure 6.33 Diagram 3.2.4.1

Similarly, Figure 6.9, the child diagram of transform 3 of Figure 6.7, also has the same net input/output data flow as transform 3.

The only exception to the rule of direct correspondence is the case of trivial reject paths. A trivial reject path is an error or reject data flow leav-

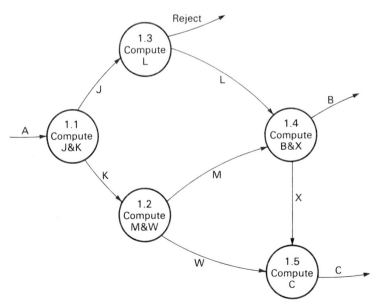

Figure 6.34

ing a process. It is considered as being trivial if no undoing of past processing is required and is simply marked reject. Furthermore, the reject path is
ignored until the main processing of the system has been documented. If an
error path does require the undoing of some past processing, then it cannot
be ignored. When a trivial error path exists, it need not be shown on the
parent transform and the child diagram. To illustrate this, Figure 6.8 has
been redrafted as Figure 6.34 and has a trivial reject path included. It can
be seen that Figure 6.34 no longer has the same net input/output data flows

Diagram Ø

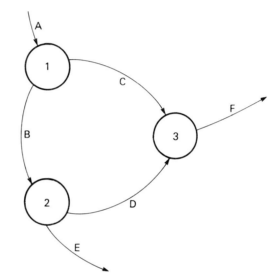

Diagram 2

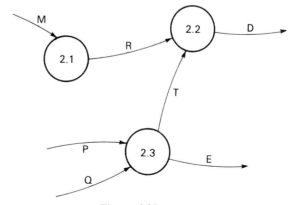

Figure 6.35

as transform 1 on Figure 6.7 but this is acceptable as it is only the trivial reject path which is upsetting the balance.

There are cases where a child diagram may appear to be out of balance with its parent transform when in fact it is not. An example of this can be seen on Figure 6.35 where diagram 2 appears to be completely out of balance with its parent transform; that is, transform 2 and diagram 2 would be in balance if it were known that data flow B consisted of data flows M, P and Q.

6.6.5 Files in partitioning

In the partitioning of DFDs a file may be shown on a child diagram which does not appear on the parent diagram. The reason for this is that the file is totally internal to the parent transform.

An example of this can be seen on Figure 6.36 where the file BOOK DATA is shown on the child diagram but is not shown on the parent. Another reason why it is shown on the child diagram is that this is the correct level to show it as, for a similar reason, data flows AA and BB are shown on the child diagram and not on the parent.

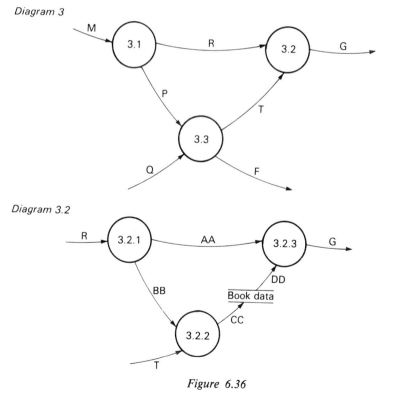

Figure 6.36

As a rule it can be stated that the level at which a file first appears is that where the file acts as a boundary between two processes. It should also be noted that on the level where the file first appears all the accesses to or from it are shown.

Referring to Figure 6.36, it can be seen that the only processes which ever use the file BOOK DATA are 3.2.2 and 3.2.3. The file would also appear on the child diagram of 3.2.2 and 3.2.3. It may also appear on the child diagrams of the child diagrams and so on.

6.6.6 Number of transforms per DFD

There is no strict rule for the number of transforms that should be shown on a DFD. It is obvious that if too many are shown on one DFD, then it will be cluttered and difficult to use. If an arbitrary number is required, then De Marco[3] offers 7 ± 2. His reason for this choice is that tests have shown that a set of seven is a number most people can cope with comfortably. However, De Marco is not saying that this is a range that *must* be used.

The main considerations in drawing DFDs is that they should be clear, readable and partitioned sensibly. What is meant by the last point is that if a system appears to require partitioning in some particular fashion, then this should be undertaken rather than stick to some strict rule as to how many transforms you are going to show on a DFD.

6.7 Summary

The term structured analysis is generally associated with:

- top-down decomposition of a system during the analysis phase
- the transformations shown in Figure 6.37
- data flow diagrams
- modularity/partitioned specification

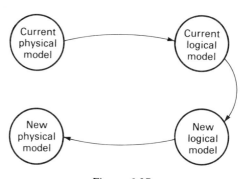

Figure 6.37

6.7.1 Advantages of structured analysis

(1) Advocates the execution of detailed analysis prior to design.
(2) Provides a tool (the DFD) which enables us to portray complex systems in simplified form.
(3) Suggests building a paper model or a blueprint of the system prior to system construction.
(4) Forces the concept of 'a place for everything and everything in its place'.

That is, we have one place (and one only) which we use to show the details/ overviews of the system.

6.7.2 Disadvantages of structured analysis

(1) Advocates detailed analysis but it would do us good to bear in mind that completeness and quickness are opposite sides of the same coin; that is, you cannot do a 'quickie' analysis and be thorough in your work at the same time.
(2) Suggests placing greater emphasis on readability, but readability and redundancy are opposite sides of the same coin; that is, to increase readability one may have to introduce redundancy.
(3) It does not solve the problem which instigated the investigation.
(4) Tedious to draft and redraft DFDs.
(5) Tedious to maintain an analysis phase DD as there is greater uncertainty regarding the details of the systems components.

In summary, although structured analysis helps you to be thorough in your job, it alone will not help you to develop information systems. There is a greater need to amalgamate its other techniques (perhaps even tradition techniques). Three points are worthy of consideration.

(1) A methodology may help you to do a job right but it does not guarantee that the right job is done![3]
(2) A methodology is a means to an end but not the end in itself.
(3) A methodology is primarily a bag of conceptual tools.

6.8 References

1. Boehm, B. W. (1976). 'Software Engineering', *IEEE Transactions on Computers*, Vol. C-25, No. 12, 1226–31, Dec.
2. Gane, C. and Sarson, T. (1979). *Structured Systems Analysis: Tools and Techniques*, Prentice-Hall.
3. De Marco, T. (1979). *Structured Analysis and System Specification*, Prentice-Hall.

4. Weinberg, V. (1978). *Structured Analysis*, Prentice-Hall.
5. Bohm, C. and Jacopini, G. (1966). 'Flow Diagrams, Turing Machines, and Languages with only Two Formulation Rules', *Communications of the ACM*, Vol. 9, No. 5, 366–71, May.
6. Beech and Burn (1967). *Trend Analysis*, Oxford University Press.
7. *Hart's Rules for Compositors and Readers at the University Press Oxford*, Oxford University Press.

6.9 Bibliography

Layzell, P. J. and Loucopoulos, P. (1986). *Introduction to Systems Analysis and Development*, Chartwell-Bratt.

Data analysis

7.1 Introduction

Planning for an information system (IS) is an activity which considers a number of related issues such as analysing the business objectives, the information needs and priorities, the functions that make up the business, the types of facts that are kept and how all these relate to each other.

Process analysis, that is the identification and modelling of the business activities, has been discussed in Chapter 5. A major component of any organisation, as it has already been emphasised, is its data and therefore the modelling of corporate data and its relationship to appropriate processes is of paramount importance for efficient planning in developing ISs. This chapter is concerned with the concepts and techniques relating to data analysis.

The importance of data analysis as an approach to information systems planning and more specifically in systems analysis and design has been recognised by many researchers and practitioners. The work of Codd[1,2] and Chen[3,4] and, very importantly, the recommendations of the ANSI/SPARC committee[5] for the design of databases, have been key milestones in the field of ISs. This work emphasises that an organisation deals with many different types of data which may have complex interrelationships. Before any attempt is made in designing and creating computer files, a thorough understanding of the data and its relationships is required. A model corresponding to this understanding, the *conceptual data model*, is an enterprise-wide model which can serve as a single reference point for all file or database structures.

A conceptual data model is a precise, unambiguous and non-redundant description of corporate data and is one of the most significant products of the data analysis process. This model encourages the IS developer to think in terms of the structure and meaning of the data in a manner which is independent of any computer or any specific file considerations. A conceptual data model is concerned with entities, their attributes and the entity relationships.

A conceptual data model is usually expressed in a diagrammatic format which greatly enhances its potential for a more accurate interpretation by non-computer specialists. This in turn provides the means for a more complete verification since a methodical approach would have been followed in understanding, classifying and organising complex information structures.

The benefit from data analysis is a better understanding of corporate data leading to a more accurate system design with the result that the computer system will be easier to maintain, easier to expand and more efficient in its performance.

Data analysis may be carried out either as a top-down or a bottom-up approach. In a top-down approach, all entities within an enterprise and their relationships are considered and described in an *entity-relationship* model. This is followed by a study known as *data normalisation* which considers individual entities and their internal relationships. Alternatively, a bottom-up approach may be followed whereby each individual entity is examined and inherent relationships within each are modelled, by carrying out data normalisation, thus eventually resulting in a complete conceptual data model.

The following activities are involved in data analysis:

(1) *Data is related to functional areas and processes.* This step defines the boundaries of study and the objectives of data analysis. Furthermore, each identified piece of data is related to one or more processes.

(2) *Entity-relationship modelling.* During this step, data is considered in more detail and findings from step (1) are refined. All identified entities and their relationships are represented diagrammatically in an entity-relationship diagram.

(3) *Functional dependency analysis.* During this step a systems developer considers individual entities and the relationships which exist within each one. These relationships may be represented diagrammatically.

(4) *Data normalisation.* Having detected any hidden relationships during step (3), data normalisation (Section 7.6) is concerned with removing these relationships so that the derived model represents the most fundamental understanding of the system. The results from this step may alter the results of step (2).

(5) *Entity life history analysis.* During this step, details about the behaviour of each entity type is documented in the form of state transition diagrams.

(6) *Integration of local data models.* Because of the complexity of most contemporary systems, a developer will normally carry out data analysis for one functional area at a time. Once all areas under examination have been covered, then data models for all the areas are integrated into one corporate data model which serves as a single reference point for all processes.

7.2 Basic constructs

Data analysis is concerned with the identification and modelling of a number of basic constructs which relate in one form or another to the composite term 'data'. It is important to understand what these basic constructs are before the process of data analysis is described.

7.2.1 Entity type

An entity is a 'thing' about which information is kept and can exist independently. An entity may be a real object, for example 'book', a concept, for example 'class session', or an activity, for example 'appointment'. An entity gives rise to entity occurrences, for example in a college there will be many occurrences of the entity 'student'. All these entity occurrences share the same properties and therefore it is convenient to think of them as belonging to the same single entity class (entity type), 'student'.

So, in a college there will be only one entity type 'student' and many occurrences for it (as many registered students).

7.2.2 Entity attributes and entity identifier

Every entity type has some properties and these are expressed in terms of attribute-value pairs. For example, a property of the entity type AUTHOR is AUTHOR-NAME and this is regarded as an attribute type which is applicable to all entities. The attribute type AUTHOR-NAME may take a value, for example 'F. Brown', and this value will correspond to a single entity occurrence, that is 'the author with the name F. Brown'. So, an attribute value is the actual data for an attribute type. All possible values for a particular attribute type are known as a domain. For example, the domain of AUTHOR-NAME is the set of all possible names.

Sometimes an entity property may be described in such a way as to result in a compound attribute. For example, the student registration form shown in Figure 7.1 contains the attribute type DATE-OF-BIRTH which is compounded by 'day', 'month' and 'year'.

NAME: ....

ADDRESS: ....

....

....

....

TEL. NO.: ....

DATE OF BIRTH: ..../............/............

Figure 7.1

Of course, this compound attribute type may be divided into its constituent parts to facilitate individual access to these parts if such a requirement
exists.

The concept of 'entity type' helps one in abstracting large volumes of
data into a top-level view of *classes of data*. For example, all authors may
be viewed in a consistent manner by considering the entity type AUTHOR
rather than individual occurrences of it. The entity type AUTHOR serves
as model of the real-world object 'author'.

Sometimes a need arises to address individual entities. This can be achieved by the use of an *entity identifier* which is one or more attribute types
whose value uniquely determines an entity occurrence. For example, the entity type AUTHOR may have as its identifier the attribute type AUTHOR-

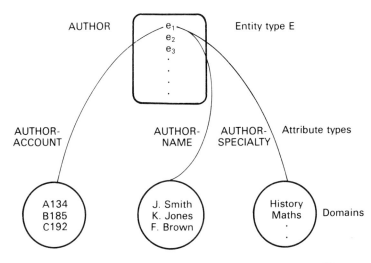

AUTHOR (AUTHOR-ACCOUNT, AUTHOR-NAME, AUTHOR-SPECIALTY)

Figure 7.2

ACCOUNT. This means that each value of AUTHOR-ACCOUNT is unique, thus enabling the exact identification of an AUTHOR occurrence.

Figure 7.2 shows the relationship between entity type, attribute type, attribute value and domain. The entity identifier is shown as the underlined attribute type.

7.2.3 Relationship type

In information systems, entity types do not exist in isolation but are related to one another. An association between two entity types is known as a *relationship type*. Consider, for example, the following statement, 'whenever a student enrolls in a course, a lecturer is allocated to this student as his personal tutor'.

At least three entity types may be identified in this statement, STUDENT, COURSE and LECTURER. The association between LECTURER and STUDENT, namely that a lecturer tutors a student, will be a relationship type and an appropriate name for it might be 'TUTORING'.

The relationships considered so far are explicit associations between entity types. In the example above, a 'conceptual link' exists between LECTURER and STUDENT as shown in Figure 7.3.

A different viewpoint of the same relationship might be a situation whereby LECTURER is regarded not as an entity type but rather as an attribute type of STUDENT as shown in Figure 7.4. Then the relationship

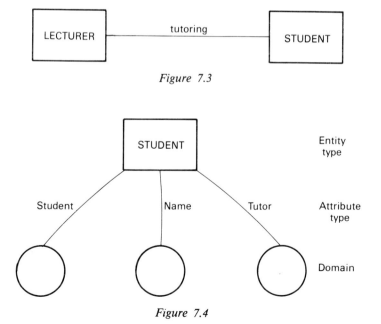

Figure 7.3

Figure 7.4

becomes implicit in the sense that a value for the attribute type TUTOR implies that the named person tutors that particular student.

The decision as to the most appropriate way of modelling relationships between different objects is very subjective and depends primarily on the understanding of the application environment by the systems developer. Data analysis is concerned with deriving models in which object relationships are as explicit as possible.

The distinction between type and occurrence that applies for entities applies also for relationships. Figure 7.5 shows occurrences of entities and relationships.

In the example of Figure 7.5 the relationship type TUTORING associates the two entity types LECTURER and STUDENT. At the occurrence level, the example shows that lecturer F. Smith tutors three students whereas K. Higgins tutors two students. In the first case there are three occurrences of relationship and in the second case two.

In order to identify a particular relationship between two entity occurrences, then the relationship identifier needs to be used. *A relationship identifier* is the composite of identifiers of the entities associated via the relationship.

There are three ways in which two objects may be related, a simple association, a complex association or a conditional association.

(1) *Simple association.* A simple association (type 1) between 'A' and 'B' exists when any value of 'A' uniquely identifies exactly one 'B'.
(2) *Complex association.* A complex association (type m) between 'A' and 'B' exists when each 'A' can be associated with any number of 'B'.
(3) *Conditional association.* A conditional association (type c) between 'A' and 'B' exists when any 'A' is associated with either one or none of 'B'.

An association between 'A' and 'B' may be shown as A→B.

A useful concept in modelling relationships between entities is that of mapping. A mapping between 'A' and 'B' is the association from 'A' to 'B' and its reverse, in other words (A→B) *and* (B→A). There are therefore the following possible mappings (1:1), (1:m), (1:c), (m:1), (m:m), (m:c), (c:1), (c:m), (c:c). In practice, the most common mappings are those of (1:1),

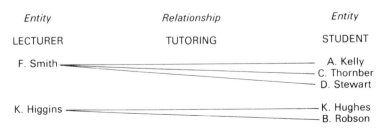

Entity	Relationship	Entity
LECTURER	TUTORING	STUDENT

F. Smith —————————— A. Kelly
—————————— C. Thornber
—————————— D. Stewart

K. Higgins —————————— K. Hughes
—————————— B. Robson

Figure 7.5

(1:m), (m:1), and (m:m). A mapping between two entity types is often referred to as the degree of relationship. The mappings are interpreted as
follows.

(1) *One-to-one mapping (1:1)*. 'For any 'A' there may be only one member
of 'B' *and* for 'B' there is only one member of 'A' associated with it.'
(2) *One-to-many mapping (1:m)*. 'For any 'A' there may be many
members of 'B' *and* for any 'B' there is only one member of 'A'
associated with it.'
(3) *Many-to-one mapping (m:1)*. 'For any 'A' there may be only one
member of 'B' *and* for any 'B' there may be many members of 'A'
associated with it.'
(4) *Many-to-many mapping (m:m)*. 'For any 'A' there may be many
members of 'B' *and* for any 'B' there are many members of 'A'
associated with it.'

The basic constructs described in this section are the fundamental blocks
of data analysis. The way the process is carried out is described in detail in
the following sections.

7.3 Relating data to processes

Data in isolation is useless unless it can be meaningfully processed.
Although data and processes can be viewed to some extent separately, it is
advantageous to relate one type of model to the other in order to derive
complete and non-redundant system specifications. Consider, for example,
the process model in Figure 7.6, illustrated by a data flow diagram (Chapter
6).

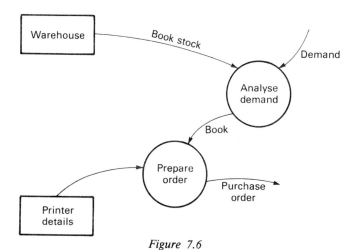

Figure 7.6

It is obvious from this simple example that a number of different entity types exist within the function 'order books out of stock'. Process analysis is not concerned with the behaviour of entity types but obviously such an understanding could only enhance the validity of the process model. Equally, understanding the behaviour of processes is an important factor in developing complete data models.

Therefore the modelling organisational processes and data are activities which should be carried out in parallel so that knowledge from one type of model is used to construct and refine the other (Figure 7.7).

Therefore, a first step in data analysis is to relate entity types to processes. The result can be shown as a matrix as in Figure 7.8. The horizontal axis of this matrix shows the processes which are involved in the business function 'purchase book' for a firm of publishers. The vertical axis records all

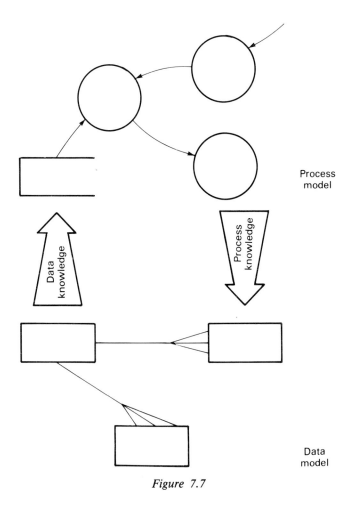

Figure 7.7

Data \ Process	Analyse demand	Identify reorder	Prepare order	Trace order	Cancel order	Check delivery	Return books	Store books	Receive invoice	Pay invoice
Book stock	X	X						X		
Warehouse	X	X				X		X		
Book	X	X	X			X	X	X		
Printer			X	X	X	X	X		X	X
Purchase order			X	X	X	X	X			
Purchase order item		X	X	X	X	X	X			
Printer terms			X	X	X	X	X			
Delivery				X	X	X	X		X	
Delivery item				X		X	X	X	X	
Payment (to printer)										
Printer invoice										X
Printer invoice item									X	X
Shipper						X				

Figure 7.8

the different types of data that exist within this business function. In practice, the distinction between different types of data is made by a systems developer who would gather information about the organisation using techniques such as interviewing relevant personnel, observing the flow of documentation etc.

7.4 Entity-relationship modelling

An entity-relationship (E-R) model is a representation of entity types and their relationships within an enterprise, in an abstract and unified manner. The model is machine independent and does not consider constraints which may be imposed by a particular file or database architecture. This model can serve not only as the means of understanding the behaviour of corporate data but also as the basis for designing and implementing file and database structures. Many of the concepts and techniques used in E-R modelling owe much to database research, mainly Chen's work.[3]

An E-R model is a collection of individual *local models* each pertaining to an application process. A *global model* is an aggregation and integration of all local models and serves as a single reference point for all processes. A high-level view of an E-R model is obtained via an E-R diagram. In order to construct an E-R model, the following steps are followed:

(1) Identify and name all entity types. No two entity types may have the same name.
(2) For each entity type, identify and name all attribute types.
(3) For each entity type, denote the attribute types which make up the entity identifier.

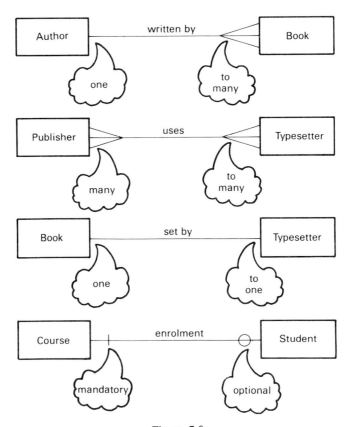

Figure 7.9

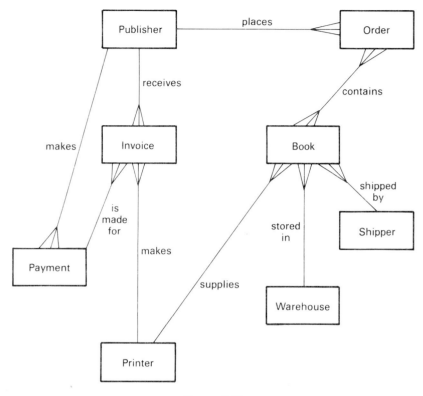

Figure 7.10

(4) Identify and name all entity relationships.
(5) For each entity type, determine its degree.
(6) Draw an E-R diagram

The steps outlined above represent an iterative process. A systems developer needs to verify results with end users, and each successive E-R diagram serves as the common basis of understanding between developer and user, thus gradually refining each previous version of the data model.

In an E-R diagram, entity types are represented as rectangles and relationships as lines connecting the participating entity types. The conventions used are shown in Figure 7.9. An example of an E-R diagram is given in Figure 7.10.

The E-R diagram in Figure 7.10 deals with the entity types and their inter-relationships for a publishing company. The reason for this particular representation lies in the way the company operates and in particular this model relates to the 'publish books' function. This emphasises the point made in Section 7.3 that a data model needs to have knowledge about the way the organisation operates, that is, knowledge of the process model. This knowledge provides the means of establishing the *context* within which data operate.

7.5 Functional dependency analysis

Functional dependency analysis is concerned with the identification and modelling of relationships between attribute types. A diagrammatic notation may be used to enhance visibility of results.

Each attribute type is represented as an ellipse and each functional

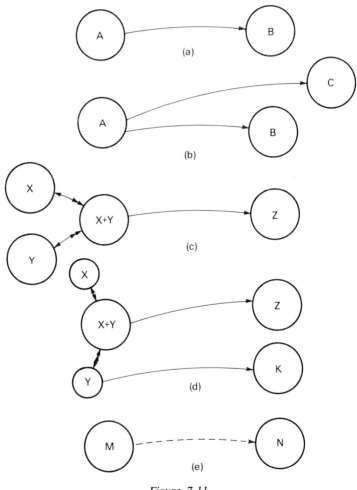

Figure 7.11

dependency (association) as a line between the two ellipses. The direction of the association is indicated by the direction of an arrow.

Consider, for example, two attribute types A and B. B is functionally dependent on A if a value of A uniquely determines the value of B. Examples of functional dependencies are shown in Figure 7.11. In 7.11(a) B is functionally dependent on A; in 7.11(b) B and C are both functionally dependent on A. In the diagrams the direction of the arrows is significant. In 7.11(a) and 7.11(b) the attribute type A is the *identifying attribute*. An identifying attribute may consist of more than one element as mentioned in Section 7.2.2. In 7.11(c) the two attribute types X and Y are required as an entity identifier. In this case Z is functionally dependent on *both* X and Y. In 7.11(d) K is functionally dependent on part of the identifier, only on Y. Finally, in 7.11(e) N is dependent on M but both are *non-identifying attributes*.

Functional dependency analysis is carried out in order to determine relationships between attribute types. This analysis is a very useful exercise in its own right but it is also an essential activity in carrying out the process of data normalisation, a process which is described in the next section.

7.6 Data normalisation

So far, data analysis has been introduced with regard to a high-level view of entities and their relationships. As mentioned in Section 7.1, it is possible to analyse data following a different (but complementary) approach whereby each entity is examined individually. For each entity, all functional dependencies are identified and then any hidden relationships are removed by decomposing the original entity into two or more entities. This process is known as *data normalisation.*

Data normalisation is a step-by-step technique of analysing data into its constituent entities and attributes. Three basic structures or 'normal forms' are usually applied although further refinements have been proposed.[6]

Figure 7.12 summarises the data normalisation process.

(1) An entity is in first normal form (1NF) if every attribute is based on a simple atomic domain. There are no repeating groups within the entity.

(2) An entity is in second normal form (2NF) if it is already in 1NF and each non-identifying attribute depends fully upon the identifying attribute.

(3) An entity is in third normal form (3NF) if it is already in 2NF and there is no dependency between the non-identifying attributes.

The technique of data normalisation is considered here with the aid of an example. Consider the form shown in Figure 7.13 which represents a purchase order for a publishing company.

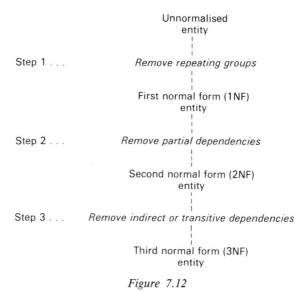

Unnormalised
entity
|
Step 1 . . .   *Remove repeating groups*
|
First normal form (1NF)
entity
|
Step 2 . . .   *Remove partial dependencies*
|
Second normal form (2NF)
entity
|
Step 3 . . .   *Remove indirect or transitive dependencies*
|
Third normal form (3NF)
entity

Figure 7.12

Order Number: 0012

Customer number: __00119__

Customer Address: __100 High Street__

__Altrincham, Cheshire__

Order Date: __10/12/86__

Delivery Date: __20/12/86__

Book No.	Book Title	Book Price	Qty Ordered	Price
7001	COBOL	10	3	30
3007	PASCAL	15	2	30
1137	DP	10	10	100
				160

Figure 7.13

In following the data normalisation process, we will consider this form as one occurrence of the entity type PURCHASE-ORDER. This entity may be represented as follows:

PURCHASE-ORDER(order-no,cust-no,cust-address,order-date, delivery-date,(book-no,book-title,book-price,qty-ordered,price), total-price).

The attribute type ORDER-NO is the entity identifier. The inner set of brackets signifies that the attribute types enclosed in them form a repeating group.

7.6.1 First normal form entities

The rule for deriving entities in 1NF is to remove any repeating groups of attribute types. Repeating groups are rewritten as new entities. In order to link the derived entities to the original entity so that information loss does not occur, the identifier of the original entity must be part of the derived entities.

In PURCHASE-ORDER there exists a repeating group and therefore this entity type is not in 1NF. If PURCHASE-ORDER is decomposed into two entity types, PURCHASE-ORDER and PURCHASE-ITEM, by removing the repeating group, then the resultant entities are shown in Figure 7.14.

For PURCHASE-ITEM the attribute type BOOK-NO is not enough to uniquely determine an occurrence of this entity type. What is required is the participation of ORDER-NO (which is incidentally the identifier of the original entity type).

The two new entity types do not have any repeating groups and therefore are in 1NF.

PURCHASE-ORDER(order-no,cust-no,cust-address,order-date,delivery-date, total-price)
PURCHASE-ITEM(order-no,book-no,book-title,book-price,qty-ordered,price)

Figure 7.14

7.6.2 Second normal form entities

The next step is to analyse the entities in Figure 7.14 to determine whether they are in 2NF. For an entity type to be in 2NF it must already be in 1NF and every non-identifying attribute type must be fully functionally dependent on the identifier.

In our example, PURCHASE-ORDER has only one attribute type as its identifier and therefore it is by default already in 2NF. Examination of the entity type PURCHASE-ITEM reveals the functional dependencies between the identifying and non-identifying attribute types as shown in Figure 7.15. This shows that BOOK-TITLE and BOOK-PRICE are only partially dependent on the identifier since a value of BOOK-NO can uniquely determine a value for BOOK-TITLE and BOOK-PRICE. Therefore the entity type PURCHASE-ITEM is not in 2NF. It can be transformed into one by decomposing it into two entity types. The total set of entity types in 2NF is shown in Figure 7.16.

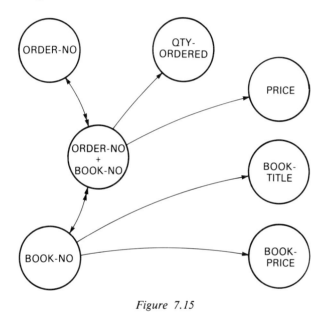

Figure 7.15

PURCHASE-ORDER(order-no,cust-no,cust-address,order-date,delivery-date, total-price)
PURCHASE-ITEM(order-no,book-no,qty-ordered,price)
BOOK(book-no,book-title,book-price)

Figure 7.16

7.6.3 Third normal form entities

The next step is to determine whether any *transitive dependencies*, that is dependencies between non-identifying attributes, exist. An entity type is in 3NF if it is already in 2NF and no transitive dependencies exist.

The reason for carrying the process beyond the 2NF stage is that a number of anomalies may occur at a later stage in the development life-

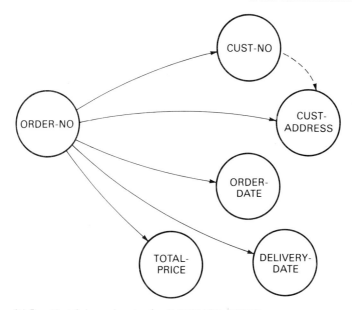

(a) Functional dependencies for PURCHASE-ORDER

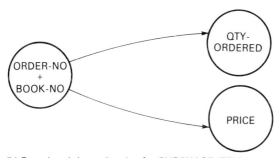

(b) Functional dependencies for PURCHASE-ITEM

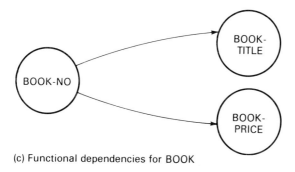

(c) Functional dependencies for BOOK

Figure 7.17

cycle. For example, consider what might happen once the system goes into operation with file structures which reflect the entity types of Figure 7.16. In this case it would not be possible to enter details of a new customer until this customer has made an order. Also, if the last record of a customer order was to be deleted, so would the customer details even though at some later stage the same customer may place new orders.

To avoid this type of anomaly, we need to decompose those entity types in Figure 7.16 which are not already in 3NF. Figure 7.17 shows all the functional dependencies for each entity type. From 17(b) and 17(c) it is obvious that entity types PURCHASE-ITEM and BOOK are already in 3NF. In 17(a) the non-identifying attribute type CUST-ADDRESS is functionally dependent on CUST-NO. Therefore, PURCHASE-ORDER is not in 3NF. It can be transformed into one by decomposing it so that the transitive dependency is removed.

The set of entity types in 3NF is shown in Figure 7.18.

PURCHASE-ORDER(order-no,cust-no,order-date,
delivery-date,total-price)
CUSTOMER(cust-no,cust-address)
PURCHASE-ITEM(order-no,book-no,qty-ordered,price)
BOOK(book-no,book-title,book-price)

Figure 7.18

7.6.4 Data normalisation and the E-R model

An E-R model is an attempt to gain a high-level understanding of corporate data. The E-R diagram is a very useful tool in documenting entity types and their associations.

As mentioned already, data normalisation is a technique for decomposing an entity type into its constituent entity types, assuming that the original entity is not in 3NF.

However, despite their apparent differences, the two approaches are very similar in that they attempt to derive atomic entity types with all entity relationships explicitly stated. In fact, the concept of entity relationship enables one to cross-check the output from the two approaches.

The commonality of view between the two approaches is demonstrated in Figure 7.19 which shows two corresponding representations for the entities of Figure 7.18.

7.7 Entity life history analysis

Entity life history (or entity life-cycle) analysis is concerned with documenting details of the behaviour of entity types in reaction to events which take place within the system under consideration. For each entity type all the

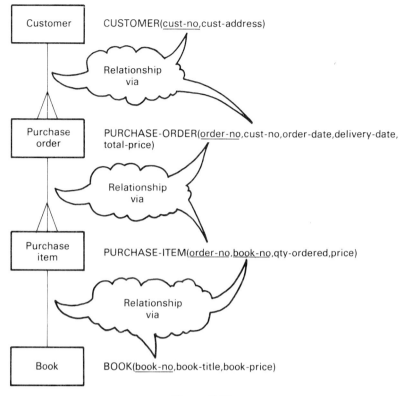

Figure 7.19

events which may affect an occurrence of it during its life are documented. The only events which are considered are those which trigger some action to take place in the system. For example, the event 'order arrives' triggers the elementary function 'process order' which can be decomposed into a number of system actions such as 'check creditworthiness', 'check stock', 'raise invoice' and so on.

The entity type ORDER may be involved in different business functions during its life depending on whether, for example, there is enough stock, the customer's credit is acceptable etc. This entity type therefore can exist in different states and this existence is guided by an event taking place.

Entity life history analysis is concerned with documenting the possible states of an entity type and the events which cause an entity occurrence to be at a particular state. To assist in this documentation one of a number of diagramming techniques may be used to show the transition of an entity's states.

The entity life history analysis is another way of relating process models to data models. This activity imposes an almost formal way of examining all processes which use a particular entity type. The advantage of the technique at the planning and analysis stage is to ensure that all possible events associated with an entity type have been considered. Furthermore, the knowledge of what processes are valid in each state of the entity type can be used during transaction system design.

As an example of an entity life history analysis, consider the case where an organisation is considering to hold a conference and has invited would-be authors to submit papers. In this case there are obviously many different processes and entity types involved.[7,8] However, just consider one entity type, that of CONF-PAPER. This may be in the following states during its life:

(1) *Intended.* This happens if a would-be author writes a letter to the organising committee to inform them that he intends to send a paper.
(2) *Contributed.* When the paper arrives.
(3) *Shortlisted.* This happens when a paper has arrived, it has been forwarded to one or more referees and has been deemed to be acceptable.

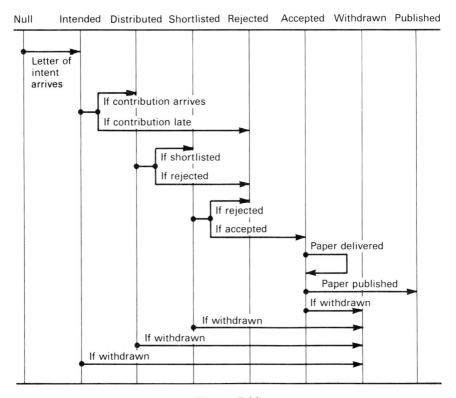

Figure 7.20

(4) *Rejected*. An occurrence of CONF-PAPER may be rejected because it was submitted late, or it was rejected by the referee.

(5) *Accepted*. This state is applicable when a CONF-PAPER has been first shortlisted, the author has been notified to this effect and a final version of the paper has arrived.

(6) *Withdrawn*. This state can be reached voluntarily by the author at any of the above states except when it is in the 'accepted' state.

(7) *Published*. A CONF-PAPER can be in this state if it has already reached the 'accepted' state.

It is obvious even from this relatively simple example that it is very difficult to use a narrative for describing the possible states of CONF-PAPER. A state transition diagram as shown in Figure 7.20 is an excellent vehicle for recording the different states of this entity type.

7.8 Integration of data areas

In order to cope with the complexity of contemporary organisational systems, an information system developer will attempt to decompose the problem space into smaller, more manageable units. The concept of decomposition for processes was extensively discussed in Chapter 6.

Since data models need to be developed in parallel with developing process models, many developers find it helpful to apply the decomposition process to data analysis. This means a developer will construct data models for individual processes or functional areas. These data models are known as local data models.

One of the advantages of carrying out data analysis is the derivation of a single data model which can serve as a single reference point for all functions. Therefore, when all functional areas have been analysed, a global data model needs to be derived. This global model is an aggregation and integration of all local data models.

7.9 Summary

Data analysis is concerned with the modelling of the static elements of an information system. The outcome of the process is a data model which is a precise, unambiguous and non-redundant representation of these static constructs. The representation of the model is in terms of E-R diagrams, functional dependency charts, normalised entity types and entity life history diagrams. Data analysis together with process analysis represents a major step in understanding user requirements for an information system and makes planning the development of such a system less of a hit-and-miss exercise.

7.10 References

1. Codd, E. F. (1970). 'A relational model of data for large shared data banks', *Comm. ACM*, Vol. 13, No. 6, June.
2. Codd, E. F. (1972). 'Further normalisation of the data base relational model', *Data Base Systems*, Courant Computer Symposia Series, Vol. 6, Prentice-Hall.
3. Chen, P. P. (1976). 'The entity-relationship model: towards a unified view of data', *ACM Trans. on Database Systems*, March.
4. Chen, P. P. (1977). *The entity-relationship model—a basis for the enterprise view of data*, National Computer Conference.
5. ANSI (1975). *Interim Report of ANSI/X3/SPARC Group on Database Management Systems*, ANSI, Feb.
6. Kent, W. (1983). 'A simple guide to five normal forms in relational database theory', *Comm. ACM*, Vol. 26, No. 2, Feb.
7. CRIS1 (1982). *Information systems design methodologies: a comparative review*, Olle, T. W. *et al.* (eds), North-Holland.
8. Macdonald, I. G. (1986). *Information Engineering: An improved, automated methodology for the design of data sharing systems*, CRIS 86 Conf. Proc., Holland, 4–7 May.

7.11 Bibliography

Tsichritzis and Lochovsky (1983). *Data Models*, Prentice-Hall.
Vetter and Maddison (1981). *Database Design Methodology*, Prentice-Hall.
Rock-Evans (1981). *Data Analysis*, IPC Business Press Ltd.
Howe, E. (1983). *Data Analysis for Database Design*, Edward Arnold.

Fourth-generation systems

8.1 Introduction

The micro revolution of the fourth generation of computing has seen the cost of computer hardware drop to such an extent that there will be a continuing growth in demand for applications in both the scientific and commercial fields. However, this rapid growth in demand presents a number of problems to potential users. Application programs developed in the traditional way take a long time to write and require the knowledge of computer professionals. These specialists are already in short supply as evidenced by the findings of the Butcher Committee and heavily outnumbered by the majority of the white-collar population. Unless programming productivity can be increased, the consequences of satisfying demand for new applications would mean an impossibly large intake of people into the computing profession and subsequently training them to program in traditional languages such as COBOL and PL/1. This would clearly be impossible, not to mention impractical.

The productivity of writing in traditional languages such as COBOL, FORTRAN or PL/1 can be improved by the use of structured techniques such as the Jackson methodology, but even these techniques do not offer the level of productivity that is required. A further problem to be considered is that the percentage of available human resources spent on developing new applications is heavily outweighed by that spent on maintaining existing systems which were developed using these languages.

The demand for new applications is rising faster than data processing (DP) can supply them. The growing backlog and inability of DP to meet project deadlines is well documented and ever increasing.

Apart from the issues of productivity and turn-round, one of the most fundamental problems with traditional methods for implementing applications is simply that the COBOL-orientated computer specialist speaks a different language to the business-orientated user. This represents a barrier to effective communication between the two. New and improved methods are required if there is to be any way of breaking out of this vicious circle.

In the past, the generation of a computer referred to the type of hardware from which it was built. The first generation of computers were built from valves and demanded a large amount of space; they also had excessive power and cooling needs. The second generation of computers used transistors instead of valves. This reduced space, power and cooling requirements as well as improving reliability. Discrete transistors were in turn superseded by integrated circuits, which formed the dominant technology of the third generation.

Manufacturers developed ways of putting groups of transistors on to silicon wafers. At first only very simple integrated circuits were made, incorporating a handful of transistors, but later more and more transistors could be laid down on a chip as the merging methods were perfected. Nowadays, chips with 100 000 transistors are not unusual, while the limit of technology approaches 500 000 transistors on a single chip. This large-scale integration may be looked upon as the fourth generation of computer technology. It is apparent that there is a distinct identifiable physical characteristic associated with the hardware of each generation.

A similar approach could be applied to explain how we arrive at the current fourth generation of computer languages, although there are many differing interpretations.

In the first generation, programs were written in machine code. The second generation was the level of assembler language, followed by the introduction of higher-level machine-independent languages such as COBOL, PL/1, FORTRAN and BASIC. In the seventies, many new facilities were introduced that may be classified as programming aids, for example, database management systems and report generators. These have increased in sophistication to become the tools of fourth-generation software development.

8.2 Fourth-generation characteristics

Many query languages, report generators, graphics packages and application generators are non-procedural in that they involve specifying what is to be done as opposed to how to do it. However, some high-level programming languages are now acquiring non-procedural capabilities. NOMAD is a high-level language with which some end users obtain fast results from a computer. For example:

LIST BY CUSTOMER AVERAGE (INVOICE TOTAL)

is a complete 'program'. It is left up to the software to decide how the list should be formatted, when to skip pages, number pages, how to sort into customer sequence and how to compute an average.

Another major attribute of fourth-generation languages is that they contain database management capabilities as an integral component. This is significantly different from the COBOL environment, where the database manager is a totally separate and often poorly integrated processing facility. A related characteristic is that the user is completely shielded from all physical database management issues. The mechanics of how and where the data is stored is not the concern of the user, nor should it be.

In investigating the problems of programmer productivity, many DP managers have discovered a strange anomaly: the more efficient the DP organisation gets at implementing applications, the more the backlog of applications seems to grow. In other words, each improvement in productivity seems to have the unfortunate effect of unleashing even more demand for new applications. Many people acknowledge that this snowballing effect in computing productivity does occur and a solution must be found.

One way to attempt to contain this effect could be to give end users the means to do as much as possible of their own data processing. Users are, by their very nature, non-DP professionals and so in order for them to be able to do more of their processing they need to be given appropriate tools.

These tools fall under the generic label of fourth-generation languages. The term 'language' should be treated with some caution as there are several other defining criteria to be considered when talking about a fourth-generation language.

Nonetheless, those systems capabilities which are now collectively designated by the label 'fourth-generation language' represent truly significant software innovations. The central idea is to give the end user all the necessary tools for building his own application.

This could create a problem in that as an increasing number of end users begin using these facilities, an ever-increasing burden is placed on computing professionals to keep up with the new pace of development.

There are several criteria that must be considered when talking about fourth-generation languages and these will be discussed in the following sub-sections.

8.2.1 Result-oriented computing

Fourth-generation languages represent non-procedural programming facilities and hence are easier for the novice to use. This is one of the most common characteristics of fourth-generation languages and one with direct relevance to the aim of improving productivity.

Under the result-orientated approach, an information problem is specified and instructions are provided for specifying the result. To create a report, for example, a table format for the data might be specified, along with break, total and heading specifications as required. No line counting or procedural looping is required, nor any 'programming' to fit the data on to the output media. Sorting is automatic. Similarly, there is no requirement for record-by-record study of the physical structure of the data held. Instead, the fourth-generation language translates the user's request into the procedural steps needed to produce the results. The user merely specifies what data or action is required, along with what form the results are to take. The method of achieving the result remains invisible to the user.

Support for result-orientated programming enables users other than full-time professionals to take advantage of the fourth-generation language.

8.2.2 Breaking down the language barrier

The most successful results in joint endeavours occur when all participants speak and understand a common language. Unfortunately, commercial DP has traditionally been practised by professionals speaking a language (COBOL or system flow charts or decision tables) foreign to those with actual information problems to solve. This means not only that end users are unable to solve simple problems themselves, but that problems must be translated into a language alien to them. This translation requires substantial time and effort and often produces results that are less than satisfactory, due to the ambiguities which inevitably arise from the translation process.

A major aim of fourth-generation languages is to eliminate this language barrier altogether. For those applications still requiring the intervention of professionals, it can be anticipated that far less about each requirement will get lost in the 'translation'.

A common language solution, however, can only work where the fourth-generation language is responsive to the level of expertise possessed by the particular user. A language suited only to the naive user would hardly suffice for the professional; conversely, a language aimed only at the professional would be likely to overwhelm the novice.

The solution lies with the concept of adaptability — the ability of the fourth-generation language through defaults and building-block techniques to respond to the user's own level of capability.

Incidentally, the user's level of interest can also be added to this since even the more sophisticated user is not necessarily interested in extensive fine-tuning simply to produce one-off or prototype results.

8.2.3 Application growth

Some applications naturally grow over time. This growth can occur in two ways: growth in capability and growth in usage.

In the fourth-generation language context, growth in capability begins with the first expression of a requirement ('I need information on . . .'), and continues throughout the life of the application. Many of these changes in demand can be accommodated by presenting the user with prototypes — systems developed quickly which indicate to the user what he can expect of the final system. It is crucial that prototypes are easy (and cheap) to create — and equally important that any defaults are 'manually' revisable.

Growth in usage means that an application that appears to be departmental is often subsequently perceived as valuable to others or 'corporate'. Effective means of sharing the application ('effective' also means retaining clear-cut lines of authority) becomes an important issue. This requires the application to be used on a shared basis, possibly by placing its components on to a central database.

8.2.4 User/machine boundary

Hardware and system software represent the internal mechanics of DP systems and thus are not important for the user of result-orientated approaches. The user of a fourth-generation language should therefore be completely shielded from any awareness of the particular hardware/systems software environment under which his applications run. From the opposite perspective, insulation from the machine environment means that applications (and their databases) should be readily portable between different systems environments. In other words, not only should the user's problem-solving ability be 'portable', but his problem-solving applications as well.

8.2.5 User environment

A fourth-generation language is not simply a language, but an interactive and integrated facility for developing applications. This means several things. The user must be able to store 'work' and then find and recall it as necessary.

For example, the intermediate data results from a partially completed problem should be easily and/or automatically put into 'temporary' storage. Requests just issued should be readily available for additional use or refinement. System facilities should also be available for finding out what work has been stored away.

8.2.6 Software support

To fully exploit the availability of computing power, the fourth-generation language user needs a variety of software tools, each capable of producing fast results. Functional needs include the following:

- tools to provide special decision-support results, for example using models
- access to required data no matter where or how stored
- reporting facilities that best emphasise the user view of the data (for example via graphics).

As with all fourth-generation language facilities, the mechanics of such tools should be transparent to users.

8.2.7 Corporate information system

The traditional approach to DP revolved around developing separate systems for individual departments. The result of this was a proliferation of individual information systems each of which takes its own individual approach to such common activities as reporting, data definition, file organisation and access. Such solutions fail to work in unison towards building a corporate management information system (MIS).

The problem facing fourth-generation languages is to allow integration consolidation and co-ordination of all system facilities such that the user always interacts with the system in a consistent manner.

Even in more traditional DP contexts, similar problems should be solved in similar ways. The modern view is that data is a corporate resource and that the MIS supports the whole organisation. It is therefore unwise to adopt the piecemeal departmental approach to its development.

One of the characteristics that most clearly distinguish fourth-generation languages from predecessors is their built-in database capability. The main requirement of this database access capability is separation of user views from the 'internal' mechanism associated with physical data storage structures. The user's views should be as simple as possible, and there should be no restrictions on what user views can be defined given the underlying structures. New views should be able to be defined fairly easily and quickly.

Additional facilities should be provided to support selective data retrieval given a particular view (this provides user-understandable specification of what data is required), as well as the ability of combining data in a controlled fashion from a number of individual user views.

8.2.8 Data dictionary environment

To make the most effective use of this type of software support system, it is necessary for end users to be able to obtain reliable, accurate and complete information about what data is stored and how it is named. With such information, the end user can formulate his own requests without the necessity for too much intervention by the professional staff.

The user must be able to access information about particular file definitions that he has created. As with any data, access to this 'meta-data' should be accommodated as far as possible through the standard facilities of the language, eliminating the need for learning any special syntax.

With corporate data, equivalent features should be offered. In addition to this, standardised data element definitions should be supported, together with the capability for providing accessible information about available data and ready-to-use procedures. Such information can help avoid the overlap and redundancy which would act as a barrier to the integration of systems into a corporate MIS.

8.3 Application development with fourth-generation systems

There are a number of categories of software support provided by fourth-generation systems. These include:

(1) *Query languages:* these are offered as database user languages which can cater for simple enquiries to retrieve or amend data. They permit the users to enter and update data and, to a limited extent, create and use personal mini databases or files.

(2) *Report generators:* whereas query languages concentrate on helping users retrieve desired data, report generators help users format information into business reports. Report generators are really an extension of the query language into more complex retrieval, processing and display. Through a report generation facility, default values will produce standard report formats or users can specify their own formats: rows, number of lines/page etc. Some generators can perform simple statistical functions such as totalling and averaging.

(3) *Application generators:* these contain modules that permit an entire application to be designed and developed by the user. The input can be specified, its validation, how it is processed and what output is created. Application generators usually operate with databases and can greatly speed up application development.

(4) *Very high-level programming languages:* these are designed so that they use a much smaller number of instructions than languages such as COBOL or PL/1 and thereby allow potentially faster development of the application. With a high-level language such as NOMAD (which operates with a relational database), the user does not have to specify every detail of procedures that are used. He can say LIST, INSERT, AVERAGE, SORT, SUM and so on. He need not describe in detailed code the format of a report. The interpreter selects a reasonable format which the user can adjust if he wishes.

(5) *Graphics interface:* some vendors are now offering software for interactive graphics that can enable users to ask for data and specify how they want it manipulated. Good examples of such systems are Apple's Lisa and Macintosh. These are operated using a mouse device which causes an arrow to be moved on the screen to point to graphic representations of files, reports etc. or indeed of a systems design.

Although much of the fourth-generation software falls into one of the above categories, a major characteristic of some fourth-generation languages is to cross the category boundaries in order to build a complete decision-support environment. A user could learn a query language and when he wishes to extend his skills to create reports, he could migrate to using a report generation facility. Some of the above languages can be called by conventional programming languages. IBM's SQL routines can be called by COBOL, PL/1 or assembler language programs.

Many products lay claim to being 'designed for end users' when in fact some degree of programming knowledge may be required, and certainly a great deal of time needs to be spent in learning the new language before being able to do anything productive or useful. In a number of cases the software is perhaps more suitable for a systems analyst who can use it to build prototype systems. These can be used as the basis for evaluating the end-user requirements.

8.4 The NOMAD language

NOMAD (note this refers to NOMAD2, the current version) is available from D and B Computing Services (formally CSS International) who have the propriety rights to it and sell the product throughout the UK and Europe.

Like some other fourth-generation languages, NOMAD has its own database management system. It combines these facilities with a report and graphics generator, and a very high-level programming language. The aim is to enable non-DP professionals to build applications using a set of simple English-like statements.

The NOMAD language incorporates both procedural and non-procedural statements. The user can operate in two modes: conversational and procedural. Users often start with conversational mode which contains non-procedural commands. These are executed interactively, one at a time, as they are issued.

A typical example of a non-procedural command would be:

LIST BY SUBJECT : TITLE, AUTHOR.

Such a command generates a report with NOMAD automatically generating page numbers and column headings, and formatting the report.

The user can generate a wide variety of reports as well as being able to add new fields, change the database structure, generate statistics and perform calculations on the data.

The full language is fairly comprehensive and can accomplish almost anything that could be done in COBOL. Most end users employ only a small sub-set of the language, and can be taught to achieve sophisticated results in a relatively short time.

Tasks which may be executed on a number of occasions can be stored by NOMAD. The user can call and execute the routine with a single statement naming the routine, for example:

SUBJECT ANL

NOMAD stores data in relational form and also in hierarchical form by means of pointers in the records, which are followed automatically when operations referring to a hierarchical structure are used. Sometimes hierarchical and relational structures are combined.

Like other database management systems, it can access data sequentially or randomly. It has features for security, integrity and for checking the accuracy of data. It has concurrency controls and locks for when multiple users have simultaneous, shared access to the data. It protects the data from system failures and uses automatic audit trails.

The structures of data are defined to NOMAD in a schema. The schema may contain column headings, alternate names for fields (aliases), details of integrity checks that are applied to the data, security controls, details of how a derived field should be computed, and details of access methods. A schema description is given in Figure 8.1.

The phrase INSERT = KEY (ID) indicates that ID is the primary key and new records are inserted using this key.

It is wasteful to store SUBJ or POSITION as twelve alphanumeric characters (as A12 implies). Department or position could each be stored as a one-character code and NOMAD could look up the meaning of the code.

MASTER AUTHOR INSERT = KEY (ID)

ITEM ID A4 HEADING 'AUTHOR: NUMBER';

ITEM AUTHOR A20 HEADING 'AUTHOR: NAME':

ITEM SUBJ. A12 HEADING 'SUBJECT'

ITEM ROYALTY £99,999 HEADING 'CURRENT: ROYALTY';

ITEM POSITION A12 HEADING 'CURRENT: POSITION';

Figure 8.1 Schema

The person who defines the file could write:

DEFINE SUBJECT A30 EXPR (DEPT DECODE (1 = 'COMPUTING',
2 = 'MATHS', 3 = 'STATS'. . . .))

NOMAD supports the following types of database access:

(1) *Keyed.* Key sequential access can be used in specifying multiple-item keys. Data can be logically ordered by the key items in ascending or descending sequence.
(2) *Table look-up.* NOMAD has a number of table look-up techniques that allow data from different masters, segments or even different databases to be combined to form a logical file.
(3) *Combined databases.* NOMAD supports the technique of combining two or more separate databases. One command, the DBADD, allows users to temporarily extract information from different databases.
(4) *External files.* Any fixed-length sequential data file can be accessed by NOMAD and can be included in the internal design of any system.

8.5 The ORACLE system

ORACLE is supplied by the ORACLE Corporation of California and comes as a complete system for accessing, manipulating and controlling all users' data. It maintains data structures in relational form, which allows any actual or logical data structure to be represented as a set of two-dimensional tables. Extra columns (or fields) may be added to a table at any time without requiring re-organisation of data or amendment to existing programs.

Any number of combinations of columns in a table may be indexed to:

● provide fast access to data based on field values
● provide multi-way selection and combination of data via the relational query language SQL
● ensure uniqueness of any combination of key fields

These factors combine to give a method of describing, manipulating and accessing data in a changing systems environment. Data independence is further provided by the idea of 'views'. The definitions of these views, together with all other data names, data descriptions and security rules, are held in a data dictionary (DD) which is an active part of the database.

The DD is also structured as two-dimensional tables and enquiries may be made on it in the same way as for other tables.

The database consists of one or more system files which may be dynamically enhanced as the system expands and in a way which is transparent to the programmer and the end user.

The system itself is a complete package and consists of the following components.

8.5.1 ORACLE kernel

This is the 'heart' of the system which controls all access to the database. It is the equivalent to a standard database management system.

8.5.2 Structured query language (SQL)

A relational language derived from the same specification as the SQL language used on IBM system.

8.5.3 User-friendly interface (UFI)

This allows the user flexibility to specify output formatting, to edit current SQL statements, to SAVE statements for subsequent re-execution and to direct output to a file for printing or further processing.

8.5.4 Host language interface

Host language interfaces are provided for COBOL, FORTRAN, MACRO-32, BASIC, PASCAL, ASSEMBLER and PL/1. These enable a program written in any of these languages to pass SQL statements to the ORACLE kernel for execution. Separate languages are not required for interactive, on-line or batch processes: SQL is the only database language used. Communication with the host language interface is via standard CALL procedures. The SQL statements in the program are interpreted at execution time by reference to the DD and, consequently, a degree of data/program independence is maintained.

8.5.5 The interactive application facility (IAG)

This is a development tool which, using a conversational dialogue approach with the designer, enables screen-driven applications to be quickly generated.

Validation, integrity checking, formatting and editing can all be simply specified without the use of traditional programming languages. The IAP executes the application under the control of the user. When generating an application interactively, the IAG conducts a dialogue with the designer to specify a new application. The designer specifies:

- field names, positions, default values, prompts and HELP messages
- validation checks for input data
- SQL statements for calculation and data processing

As the dialogue progresses, it is stored in a file. By editing this file of responses, existing applications can be modified or new similar applications created.

To simplify the user's job, interaction with the screen processor is via specially designated keys that are common to all applications. Help on the function of all keys is available.

8.5.6 Loader

This utility enables the fast loading of bulk data on a standard file into a defined ORACLE database structure. It is a tool for system conversion and can help reduce implementation costs.

8.5.7 Report writer

ORACLE provides report formatting and printing capability using the ORACLE report writer. SQL is used within the ORACLE report writer to extract data from the database and a variety of sequencing and formatting facilities are used to direct the layout and printing of the report. Column heading and data formats are taken from the DD.

Requests for totals and other calculations can be made on control breaks, report and column headings altered, page size specified, column justification etc.

To produce a report, the user prepares a control file which surrounds SQL statements with sequencing and text formatting commands.

8.5.8 Data dictionary

The ORACLE data dictionary (DD) is integrated in that as new tables, users etc. are added to the database the dictionary is automatically updated. The dictionary itself consists of a number of separate tables, which can be queried, manipulated and modified through the use of SQL.

Any changes made to the database structure are immediately entered in the DD. To obtain the names of all tables in the DD, the user can enter an SQL query.

SELECT * FROM SYSCATALOG

8.5.9 SQL language

ORACLE'S data language is SQL which is based on IBM's SQL/DS. SQL was first introduced by the ORACLE Corporation in June 1979 with a few extensions. It is a non-procedural language integrating data definition, manipulation and query functions which are often separated in other products. The language is employed by all users, in all usage environments, to perform ORACLE functions. Thus, a user, programmer or database administrator who works with ORACLE needs to learn only one language.

Statements are 'free format' with multiple clauses entered on one line or individually spread over a number of lines. Frequently-used combinations of SQL statements can be stored and executed by entering any defined sequence of characters as a single command in a similar way to setting up an external sub-routine in PL/1. In addition, SQL statements can be stored with imbedded ask-variables; a user who executes such a statement is automatically prompted to enter values for the variables. This feature makes it possible to write SQL statements for use by individuals who have no understanding of SQL.

8.6 The RAMIS system

RAMIS II is supplied by Mathematica Products Group who were one of the first DBMS vendors to pioneer an easy-to-use non-procedural language interface to the user. RAMIS has been available since the mid-1970s and was used extensively in British Telecom for *ad-hoc* management computing. The early versions tended to require large-capacity main memory and used a great deal of processing power. However, these problems have largely been rectified.

RAMIS II is a fourth-generation language and DBMS designed as a complete business information processing system. There are a number of optional modular components of RAMIS II, including a report writer, graphics and relational capabilities which are designed to operate as a unified system.

The modular structure of RAMIS II could enable an organisation to configure a system that is suited to its present needs and to extend this as needs change and applications evolve.

The components of RAMIS II generally fall into the following four functional categories:

(1) *Data access:* these components provide access to both RAMIS II databases, as well as read-only access to other types of data sources.
(2) *Data maintenance:* these components provide updating capability of RAMIS II files.
(3) *Data utilisation:* these permit the conversion of stored data into the information required to solve user needs.

(4)   *User environmental support:* these components provide a work environment for the above functions to enable development of applications by users of differing levels of sophistication.

RAMIS II files may be stored as either host files, containing both stored data and 'virtual' data, or as associated files, containing only stored data. A 'host' file is related at one of its hierarchical levels (called a 'virtual' level) to a given level of another file, called 'associated' file. Data from the associated file is available within the host file 'view' as if it were within the same file. Access to these views is based on lists of element names. The user is unable to update 'virtual' data, but must access the distinct associated file to perform the actual update. This requires some degree of file awareness by the user. In RAMIS II terminology, a 'database' refers to one or more complete applications (not to any one of the file views), including an active file dictionary, a request library and data storage. All access to RAMIS II databases is provided by the database manager who also enforces security (to the field or record level) and is responsible for ensuring file integrity.

All data accessed by RAMIS II, whether stored in a RAMIS II database or elsewhere, is defined in a file dictionary called RAMASTER. This file dictionary describes fields (including validation rules and display formats), file structures and interfile linkages. Since it is a RAMIS II file itself, standard RAMIS II language facilities are used to access and display it. Any new entries, updates and deletions are automatically directed to RAMASTER for dictionary maintenance.

RELATE is a data manipulation tool for combining data from different sources, whether RAMIS II or other. It provides a request-based method for defining relationships between data, emphasising dynamic 'relational' joins. All relational operations — selection, projection, join, division, union, intersection, set difference, exclusion and Cartesian product — are provided. With RELATE, any data (normalised or unnormalised) can be manipulated and associated.

A records management component handles most maintenance of RAMIS II files, and provides commands used to add, modify and delete records. Processing can be carried out in either batch or on-line mode. Data validation is achieved automatically using the file definition. Additional validation is applied through IF...THEN...ELSE tests and can include table lookups and access to values in other RAMIS II files. Transaction logs are provided to capture all accepted/rejected transactions, or specific types of rejected transactions.

A formatted screen manager provides facilities for building user-defined screen-based applications. The user may develop screens either using a command set based on non-procedural syntax or by drawing the layout on the screen and then defining the display and validation attributes using menus. Up to twenty-five attributes can be specified for each field including display attributes such as colour or blinking. Three validation attributes (NUMERIC, REQUIRED, MUST FILL) are available. NUMERIC causes alphabetic or special characters to be rejected. REQUIRED indicates that a transaction will not be accepted unless a value is entered, and MUST FILL indicates that when a value is entered, it must completely fill the entry blank. One other attribute is STOP WHEN FULL. This controls the terminal's action when a blank has been filled. It inhibits automatic tabbing to the next blank, and prevents accidental continuation of a value into the next blank.

The RAMIS II procedural language interface provides support to RAMIS II for application programs written in COBOL, PL/1, FORTRAN or Assembler. CALLS are made using field-level requests, and this helps to maintain data independence.

The reporter component provides support for producing tabulated reports, creating entirely new files, and providing data to other RAMIS II facilities. With the reporter, records can be selected from a file, extended with newly-defined fields, sorted, summarised and produced at a terminal or printer.

A report can be produced automatically without any prior formatting specification. The default format is easily altered through commands to rearrange the display, add annotations or modify virtually any other feature. The reporter also allows stored data to be supplemented with constructed data calculated from single or multiple values in the file. Constructed data can be specified in several ways; in many cases, the reporter has a summary operator that can be used with a field name in the request. These operators include minimum, maximum, average, total, per cent etc., as well as cumulative and statistical operations.

The plot component provides graphics reporting for data obtained through the reporter. It can generate high-resolution bar charts, histograms, line graphs, point plots and pie charts. A number of displays can be produced from a single data retrieval, and formatting commands are provided to give user control over colour and shading patterns.

The financial planning option permits a financial model to be constructed and stored as a RAMIS II database. The model can then be run in conjunction with plugged-in values to test 'what if' questions against stored data, to produce reports in financial statement format, and to provide the equivalent of a typical spreadsheet capability.

RAMIS II provides a complete work environment. The tools that make up this environment speed up the development of requests and provide assistance for less experienced RAMIS II users.

The executive consists of a control language that permits the packaging of RAMIS II non-procedural language statements into 'applications', which can be catalogued for storage into a library, then recalled by name for subsequent execution. The executive also supports substitution of values for variable parameters, dummy execution, prompting and construction of dialogues, via menus or other terminal displays, between the user and an application. Screens defined under the screen manager may also be used under the executive for support of prompting and menu-based option selection.

An interactive request modification component allows requests to be entered, tested, modified (that is, edited) and catalogued entirely within the RAMIS II environment on an interactive basis. When an error is found, RAMIS II displays a message and allows the user to correct it and continue processing, abandon the request or get assistance by entering HELP. Following the correction, the request is completed with the word END and a report is produced.

Request modification enables requests to be altered or extended to fill additional needs. Typically, changes may be required to alter the format or presentation of a report or to vary its content or the level of summarisation.

The original form of RAMIS II was called RAMIS and was introduced as one of the first non-procedural programming languages as far back as 1967. To make the access to information easier, MPG announced an improved product in 1983 as an integrated adjunct to RAMIS II. MPG have marketed this product as 'the first fully practical natural language comprehensive system'. To obtain information directly from a wide variety of computer fields, questions or requests can be made in 'everyday English'. If a request is not clear, the system tries to resolve its uncertainty by offering a paraphrase of the original request and asks the user to either confirm the systems interpretation or restate the question more clearly. The knowledge base of RAMIS II English has been designed using three dictionaries: a general dictionary of the English language that contains a basic vocabulary; RAMASTER, the RAMIS II active file dictionary containing information about files and fields; and optional file-specific dictionaries that can contain specialised terms unique to an application user.

The key difference between RAMIS II English and other English and other artificial intelligence products is that RAMIS II English is integrated into the RAMIS II system. This means English can accommodate both simple natural-language queries and standard RAMIS II Report language for the more complex reports.

Examples of such requests are:

I'd like a student list
Show me our royalty payments broken down by author across year

8.7 Prototyping

Prototyping mainly aims at increasing the productivity of system development staff, not so much in making them produce more work but in making their time more effective.

One of the great advantages of prototyping is in reducing the need for and cost of maintenance and reprocessing. According to IBM, it could cost as much as 1000 times to amend a system post-implementation as during development. Prototyping can be useful if real financial benefit can be had through early system implementation even if the running costs have not been optimised. Other benefits include better achievement of user requirements and hence higher user satisfaction, better user communication and user education as well as education for the DP staff.

Prototyping advocates developing a simple system that is refined through an interactive process. The basic steps are as follows:

(1) Identify user's basic needs in term of information and operating requirements.
(2) Develop a working prototype that performs only the most important identified functions using a small representative database, possibly with real data.
(3) Allow the user to use the prototype by demonstrating how it works and responds to requested changes.
(4) Refine the prototype by discussing requested changes and deciding which ones should be included in the next version. After the next version is created, steps (3) and (4) are repeated until the system fully achieves the requirements of the user.
(5) At some point, a decision may be made to discard the prototype, having learnt what is needed, and initiate a formal system development process. Alternatively, the prototype may become the production system.

Most prototypes do not encompass the entire system. Most gains can be achieved by concentrating on the complex part of it, which means that the prototype should consider a partitioned data model as its basis rather than a functional sub-system. This distinction is important since a functional sub-system may require the entire data model which would make the notion of prototyping invalid. It is not unusual for a data model to contain many hundreds (or even thousands) of entity types. Much time and resources will then need to be spent to develop and implement such a data model.

Before any form of prototyping is undertaken, it is important that data analysis has been carried out. Also an overall understanding of the system's functions and the flow of data between them would be useful.

It is very important that a prototype should be quick to develop and easy and cheap to change. Preferably it should be something which does not require compilation and batch turnround not only because this takes time but because it causes the loss of momentum and motivation important in iterative processes. Run-time costs are a less important consideration. It is useful if a software package is capable of supporting a top-down design, such that the overall system can be tested without having to define the lower-level programs.

The type of software described in previous sections of this chapter closely reflect that which is necessary for effective prototyping.

8.8 User participation in developing an MIS

The introduction of computer-based information systems into an organisation can change drastically the way many operations are carried out. An organisation may be affected technically, economically and behaviourally. This section deals with the important behavioural aspects associated with the introduction of a computer system. A change may be ideal in terms of a technical and economic sense but, unless it accommodates human expectations and alleviates human fears, this change will never be successful.

The rapid advances of technology in the twentieth century have had a profound effect on the way people regard 'change'. Change is observed in our everyday life at many levels, usually due to the dynamic output of technological advances, for example many new automobile models are introduced every year and readily accepted by the general public.

In an organisation, any aspect of its operation must be regarded as a logical target for change.

Change may be good or bad. But whereas the appropriateness (or not) of a change may be easy to identify with regard to technical and economical considerations, this may not be so from the behavioural point of view. What may be regarded as good by some people might be totally unacceptable to others.

An analyst must be aware of a number of strategic variables relating to the introduction of a change whether for a computer system or operating procedures. For example, it must be explained to people 'why' a change is needed or wanted. The emotional barrier that people have against changing something that they are familiar with must also be regarded in trying to implement some change. Finally the analyst must be aware that people perceive change differently.

In organisations, the introduction of a computer-based information system affects both its formal and informal structures. Any information may change departmental boundaries and job descriptions (the formal structure) as well as social and group relations (the informal structure). If these factors are not considered and dealt with as the system is being developed, resistance in the form of aggression, projection or avoidance may result.

Aggression is some form of attack on the system with the intent of making it either physically inoperative or ineffective.

Projection is a way of blaming the system for any malfunction encountered while using or interacting with it.

Avoidance is the withdrawal of people from interacting with the information system. This may be the result of frustration which may, for example, be generated from not knowing how to input some data on the computer, and this may generate avoidance. Avoiding the VDU means avoiding frustration.

Avoiding or minimising user resistance is one of the most difficult problems in introducing information systems. While an analyst knows what techniques and tools to use in order to develop an efficient system, he is not so well equipped with solving behavioural difficulties. However, the following points should be considered when a new information system is introduced.

(1) Consider how changes in the past were implemented.
(2) Discuss the system with all persons (or representatives of them) directly affected by it.
(3) Set realistic goals.
(4) State objectives clearly.
(5) Design a user-friendly system
(6) Involve end users at all stages of development.
(7) Develop a system which is reliable.

One approach to minimising user resistance is the 'participative approach', whose proponents recommend the active involvement of users in the development of an MIS.

The involvement of users in the development and implementation of systems has come about because of:

● user dissatisfaction with implemented systems
● greater industrial democracy
● the spread of humanistic values

Two reasons are put forward in support of user participation:

(1) *The management view.* The wish to harness the skills and knowledge of the participants leading to greater efficiency.
(2) *The workers' view.* The wish to protect the interests of the participants leading to job protection.

User participation in the development process can be examined in terms of:

(1) The role the user plays in the process.
(2) The stage in the life-cycle at which the user gets involved.

The role of the user in the design process may be

(1) *Consultative.* Ideas are presented to the user by an expert who notes his responses.
(2) *Representative.* Selected users join the design teams.

(3) *Consensus*. Interest groups take over the design. Experts are just but an interest group who ensure that the design is technically sound.

Involvement of the user may happen at any or all of the following major stages:

(1) Initiation of project — very unlikely. Usually only higher management is involved in this.
(2) Defining the objectives of the system.
(3) Analysis and description of existing system together with the identification of problem areas.
(4) Design of alternative solutions.
(5) Feasibility study and evaluation of alternative solutions.
(6) Detailed design of a computer system.
(7) Detailed design of a human work system.
(8) Preparation of system specification.
(9) Construction of formal computer system.
(10) Construction of human work system.
(11) Implementation of system.
(12) Evaluation of working system.

The participative approach to systems analysis advocated mainly by Mumford, Land and Hawgood[1] is gaining a lot of interest mainly because of the dissatisfaction of users with implemented systems or because of the reluctance or slowness in accepting new systems.

The participative approach is not a revolutionary one. It makes sure that the implementation stage of a computer project is acceptable to the users. This can be achieved by letting users design the user/machine interface.

However, for truly participative systems development, the user must participate in the decision-making process and additionally in the stage which led to the decision-making point.

8.9 DP staff: impact of fourth generation

In an earlier section we spoke about the generations of computer technology which have covered the thirty or so years of electronic data processing. Many of the standard techniques and applications evolved over the first three generations resulted in medium to large-scale organisations setting up self-contained data processing departments. Although the structure of the DP department varies from organisation to organisation, the same job titles and functions tend to crop up: installation managers, operators, systems analysts, system designers, programmers etc. The fourth generation has seen more of a revolutionary change rather than the evolution of previous generations and this revolution has been the real involvement of the end user in the computing process. Personal computers are becoming less of a novelty and more of a standard piece of office equipment; networks allow large amounts of data and information to be passed quickly and accurately between computers; software is now geared towards the user specifying his own system in everyday language and building that system.

These developments obviously affect the end user and their management but are also bound to affect the role of the DP professional. No longer can the user be dictated to in jargon and given systems which do not meet his requirements.

8.9.1 The fourth-generation developments

The 1980s have seen the development of information technology on a number of fronts, primarily:

- hardware
- communication
- software

Hardware

We are firmly in the age of the personal computer (PC). To clarify exactly what we are talking about, the term 'personal computer' will be used to describe a single-user desk-top computer with its own disc storage and possibly a printer. Large-scale integrated circuit technology has seen the emergence of a number of very powerful PCs, notably the IBM PC, ICL PC, DEC Professional, Apple, Commodore etc. Such systems can comfortably store millions of characters of information (on Winchester-type disc units) and perform complex DP at very high speed.

As well as the PC, the 1980s have seen the emergence of the mini-computer from the obscurity of scientific or technical computing into the business and commercial environment. Machines which comfortably support two dozen simultaneous users can run in a normal office without requiring special environmental conditions. The DP requirements of an office or a department can now be met by its own relatively cheap machine rather than by a centralised mainframe in the DP department.

Communications

The computer network is now an economically viable proposition. Advances in telecommunications and software technology have made it relatively easy and cheap for two or more computers to 'talk' to one another. The modern form of data communications, known as packet switching, has allowed standards to be developed and protocols to be specified which allow machines of different type and even different manufacture to be connected together into a network.

Packet-switching networks exist in many countries (UK, France, Germany, USA) which allow data to be transmitted at phenomenal speeds from one end of the country to the other. Moreover, gateways are provided to connect the different networks together to allow a computer in London to communicate with one in New York or San Francisco.

As well as these wide area networks, users can now take advantage of local area network (LAN) technology. A LAN can connect together computers, disc units, printers within a building on to a kind of data ring main which allows data to be passed from one machine to another and allows several machines to share resources such as discs and printers.

The next few years should see moves towards even greater standardisation. LANs will be connected to other LANs and networks of networks will be connected via wide area networks. Voice transmission (telephoning) will also become digital and will share the data circuits with video transmission.

Software

Fourth-generation software falls into a number of distinct categories: database query languages and report generators; application generators; decision support systems; code generators.

(1) *Query languages and report generators.* Modern approaches to DP tend to regard data as an organisational resource not to be tied to any particular department or application. This approach necessitates that data be stored in a database in such a way that special database management software can extract any part of the data held and present it to an application program. This has been exploited by fourth-generation software which will allow any user who has access to the data to retrieve it using simple English-like commands (query language).

SELECT SALARY
        FROM EMPLOYEE
        WHERE NAME = 'CLARE'

SELECT NAME
        FROM EMPLOYEE
        WHERE MANAGER = 'PAYNE'

Other fourth-generation software allows the user to specify reports to be produced without having to write the programs.

IN STUDENT FILE, LOOK FOR DEBTORS GREATER THAN OR EQUAL TO 100; ORDER OUTPUT BY GRANT AUTHORITY; LIST NUMBER, DEBT, NAME AND TOTAL OVERDUE FEES FOR EACH GRANT AUTHORITY.

(2) *Application generators.* These are packages which allow a user to define the data which is to be held for a particular application together with the processing which is required. The system then forms the necessary computing instructions and stores them ready for subsequent use. Although prototypes have been around for some time, application generators which are easy to use require sophisticated graphics software so that the user can see the relationship between data items being built up. Although the resultant systems tend to be more machine-inefficient than equivalent systems developed in conventional ways, they can be produced in around one-tenth of the time *and* by the end user.

(3) *Decision support systems.* This family of software enables the user to perform various management-science calculations using concise easy-to-learn commands. In the micro market, Visicalc, Supercalc and Lotus 1-2-3 are good examples. Spreadsheets can be set up, data entered and various functions specified to act on rows and/or columns.

(4) *Code generators.* Unlike the previous three groups, code generators are more for use by computer professionals. They allow access to stored data and processing formats and generate sections of COBOL or PL/1 code which can be used as skeleton programs. The programmer amends or enhances the skeleton to the complete program.

8.9.2 The information centre

From the above, it can be seen that much of the fourth-generation technology is geared towards bringing computer power to the user and away from the large DP departments. Many of the information requirements of individual functional units within the organisation will be met by the users developing their own systems on their own machines. Departments will evolve their own 'information centres' which will provide reports and information on which decisions can be based.

Although these developments are both natural and exciting, a number of problems can arise:

(1) The initial applications developed (as part of the user self-training) will be necessarily simple. However, as he becomes more confident, ambition can overtake expertise and subsequent applications become more difficult, requiring some form of consultative support.

(2) Departments rarely work in total isolation and information has to be passed from one department to another. Users given a completely free hand may tend to work in isolation and set up data incompatible with that required by other information centres.

(3) Data is a corporate resource and not the property of any one individual or department. It should therefore be accessible to all users, given appropriate security and privacy considerations. Some interface with

corporate computers and databases is inevitable, and so some form of standardisation is required.

(4) There will always be a need for 'production' DP systems which can quickly process vast amounts of data — for example, rate invoices, payroll etc. These will always require specialist design/programmer skills to make the most efficient use of computer resources.

8.9.3 The DP department

Traditionally the DP department has been responsible for all the computerised data processing and management information systems of the organisation. If the organisation moves towards fourth-generation technology, the role of the DP department must change, as will its structure. Most have the following groups of staff:

(1) *Installation staff.* Under the computer centre manager(s) are staff concerned with data preparation, operations (often on a shift basis), system software development and maintenance, hardware maintenance, data communications.

(2) *Systems analysis staff.* Usually in project teams along with systems designers and programmers, systems analysts investigate functional areas of an organisation with a view to proposing computerised systems which will satisfy the information requirements of those areas.

(3) *Systems design staff.* Using the requirements specified by the analyst, they formulate these into the design of a computer system which will meet those requirements, preparing a system specification.

(4) *Programmers.* These people work from systems specifications to develop the appropriate code to run on the computer. The coded program forms the basis of the computerised information system, which also will incorporate full documentation.

(5) *Application maintenance staff.* Computer systems always require maintenance and enhancement if they are to remain effective and efficient. Maintenance staff can be analyst/designers and programmers.

In addition to these, other staff may be concerned with disc and tape libraries, training, recruitment etc. Organisations which use the database approach will also have staff involved in database administration, whose job it is to look after the database and its associated software.

From the above it can be seen that the bulk of the staff of a large DP department are involved in project teams concerned with applications development: the very area that the fourth generation is giving to the users. So what becomes of the DP staff?

8.9.4 Fourth-generation DP departments

Many organisations have yet to move into the fourth generation. When they do, however, it does not mean the death of the computer specialist. There will be three main areas where DP staff (albeit a different breed) will be required.

(1) *Information centre consultants.* As users are provided with their own computing power, they will obviously require training in its selection and use. In addition to this, as the user graduates through levels of sophistication, he/she will require consultancy services from a specialist in the use of the particular hardware or software. A team of information centre consultants will be required either centrally or dispersed to the functional departments to provide this support and backup.

(2) *Data managers.* The importance of standardisation in the structure and naming of data used by the organisation and its information centres was stressed earlier. Some form of data dictionary will be required (possibly interfacing with the organisational database) which defines all the data held in all the information centres and on the main database. When users' machines are networked together and data passed between them there should be no problem of lack of standardisation or protocol.

(3) *Production DP staff.* There will always be a need for 'traditional' DP staff to develop, run and maintain the 'production' DP systems. These are the systems which process large amounts of data (such as invoice generation, stock control) and/or which cross departmental boundaries (payroll, staff statistics etc.). COBOL will probably still be alive and kicking in the 1990s.

8.10 Reference

1. Mumford, E., Land, F. and Hawgood, J. (1978). 'A participative approach to the design of computer systems', *Impact of science on society*, Vol. 28, No. 3.

8.11 Bibliography

McCracken, D. (1980). *A Guide to NOMAD for Applications Development*, Addison-Wesley.
Martin, J. (1983). *An Information Systems Manifesto*, Savant Tech. Report 33.
ORACLE Technical Reference Manual.
RAMIS Technical Reference Manual.

Index